THE PILLAR HOUSE COOKBOOK

The
PILLAR HOUSE
Cookbook

David Paul Larousse
AND
Alan R. Gibson

THE HARVARD COMMON PRESS
Harvard and Boston, Massachusetts

The Harvard Common Press
535 Albany Street
Boston, Massachusetts

Printed in the United States of America

Library of Congress Cataloging-in-Publication Data

Larousse, David Paul, 1949–
  The Pillar House Cookbook.

  Includes index.
  1. Cookery.   2. Pillar House (Restaurant)   I. Gibson, Alan R., 1960 –
II. Title.
TX714L37   1988   641.50974461   88-21466
ISBN 1-55832-005-9

Cover drawing by Howard L. Rich
Cover design by Joyce C. Weston
Text design by Linda Ziedrich
Color photography by Susan Wetherell and Ken Perham,
with technical assistance from Lynn Holden
Food styling, how-to illustrations, and black and white photography
by David Paul Larousse

For Carolyn and George Larsen,
founders of the Pillar House Restaurant,
and for you, our guests,
in gratitude for your ongoing loyalty and enthusiasm

T.H.L.

For Harold Chauncey Rouse
Master of sleight of hand, world-class organist,
friend, and gentle soul
1901–1986

D.P.L.

CONTENTS

FOREWORD

In June of 1987 Alan Gibson and David Paul Larousse approached me with the idea of creating a Pillar House cookbook. It was an idea I had considered for several years, and this seemed like the perfect time to embark on such an undertaking.

Ours is unique among restaurants. Those familiar with the Pillar House and its reputation know our special history and philosophy enhance the dining experience we offer. By sharing our recipes, along with some behind-the-scenes insight into what makes the Pillar House what it is, we have endeavored to send some of this dining pleasure home with you.

My father, George Larsen, started his first restaurant after owning a couple of gas stations, one of which was adjacent to a Howard Johnson's. Watching business thrive next door, he decided to open his own Howard Johnson's in Boston. After a few successful years, he sold the Howard Johnson's to start the Tudor Village restaurant, where he spent several years developing his own style as a restaurateur.

In the late forties he opened the Tobey House, a small, home-style restaurant that became well known for its exceptionally fine apple pie. Even with its homey atmosphere, the Tobey House reflected my father's appreciation for quality. Encouraged by his success, he sought larger quarters in which he could expand his clientele. He ultimately moved to the historic Curtis House, in Newton Lower Falls. A family residence since its construction in 1828, the Curtis House had been vacant for several months. After two years of renovation and restoration, the doors of the Pillar House were opened to the public on August 19, 1952.

Though I was still in school, my own involvement with the restaurant began immediately. I worked in many different capacities during my summer breaks. In 1958, upon graduating from Michigan State University with a degree in hotel, restaurant, and institutional management, I was finally able to pursue my career full time. I have been with the Pillar House ever since.

My father oversaw the innermost workings of the restaurant operation while my mother, Carolyn Larsen, established the atmosphere of the dining room. With a goal of creating a pleasant environment in which guests could relax and enjoy fine food, she trained the staff and set the standard of gracious dining. Like my father, she upheld the highest standards of excellence.

From the start I shared my family's devotion to quality. Once I took over the full-time operation of the restaurant from my parents, attention to fine details, both in the dining rooms and the kitchens, became my responsibility. I have consulted interior designers, lighting specialists, floral decorators, and a range of other professionals over the years, and have acquired considerable peripheral skills in addition to my college food service training. Because of the focus on quality, the Pillar House has developed a loyal clientele while continuously attracting those patrons seeking something new and different. Our striving for excellence has led to improvements not only in our cuisine and ambiance, but in basic policies as well.

During our first twenty years in business we were open six days a week. In 1972 I was inspired to try to make life a little more pleasant for our staff by closing on weekends. Our critics thought we were insane. Closing on the busiest days of the week, Saturdays and Sundays? Unheard of. But the results were surprising. We attracted a superior personnel, people who appreciated free time on weekends and showed it by providing better service to our patrons. When I examined the effects of the new policy, I found our revenues had actually increased since its adoption. We have maintained the Monday-through-Friday schedule ever since, and its effect on the staff's morale is even more rewarding than that on our books.

A little over ten years later, I was inspired with another idea to improve the quality of life at the Pillar House. I had become increasingly health-conscious, and it became clear to me that noxious smoke from cigarettes was really detracting from an otherwise pleasant atmosphere. So in 1986 we made the Pillar House an entirely non-smoking establishment. We've lost a few regular patrons because of this decision, but in their place are a healthier, more sophisticated group who appreciate a truly wholesome ambiance.

Over the course of my thirty-five-plus years at the Pillar House, I have also seen the menu evolve, from the traditional preparations of well-loved entrées to the more imaginative yet equally appealing cuisine that is fashionable today. We have always insisted, however, on serving only fresh and chemical-free food.

Though it has taken us all these years to finally sit down and compile a collection of Pillar House recipes, I am very proud of our achievement. It has been an honor to entrust this undertaking to both chef Alan Gibson and David Paul Larousse, an accomplished chef in his own right as well as a veteran author. Thanks to their dogged persistence and powers of persuasion, the Pillar House Cookbook has become a reality.

I hope you will enjoy our book as much as I have enjoyed watching it come to fruition.

TOM LARSEN

ACKNOWLEDGMENTS

We wish to acknowledge the following individuals and offer sincere thanks for their assistance in the creation of *The Pillar House Cookbook*.

- Bill Magnan, computer wizard extraordinaire, who set us up on a word processing system. Without his assistance, we'd still be typing the manuscript.
- Betty Pearlstein of Glassworks (814 South Aiken Avenue, Shadyside, Pittsburgh, Pennsylvania 15232), who donated some of the magnificent plates and flatware upon which we photographed the finished food items.
- Peter Van Renssalaer Rhein of Chef Services, Boston, who introduced us to Bruce Shaw, our publisher.
- Joanne Bianchi, Christopher Gatto, Mark Gunderson, and all the members of the culinary brigade at the Pillar House, who assisted us in our effort to compile this manuscript. Special thanks to David Hernandez, pastry chef, who belongs to nearly all the items in the dessert section.
- Our purveyors: Robert Ablondi and Norman Bean of United Restaurant Supply, Sid Goldman and Rick Lazaris of Old Colony Packing, Nick Katsiroubas of Katsiroubas Brothers Produce, Captain and Kim Marden and Stu James of Captain Marden's Seafood, and Ron Savenor of Savenor's Market in Cambridge. Special thanks to Michael Satzow, president of North Country Smokehouse, Claremont, New Hampshire.
- Linda Ziedrich, for her editorial and design excellence.
- Bill Pioppi and Francis Dusza of Russell Harrington Cutlery, Southbridge, Massachusetts.
- Rick Marchetti of the Ceramic Tile Factory Outlet, Warwick, Rhode Island.

"GIVE IT TO 'EM
UP TO GREEN RIVER"

One of the sponsors of this book is the Russell Harrington Cutlery Company, in Southbridge, Massachusetts. Still a leader in the American cutlery manufacture, Russell Harrington has a long and fascinating history.

In 1818, ten years before Allen Crocker Curtis built the home that would become the Pillar House restaurant, Henry Harrington Sr. began manufacturing cutlery out of a shed behind his house in Southbridge, Massachusetts. From this humble start, Harrington Cutlery eventually grew into a major manufacturer of not only cutlery, but razors, edged tools, surgical instruments, and guns.

In 1834, in the town of Greenfield, Massachusetts, another man was about to go into the cutlery business. While reading Zachariah Allen's *The Practical Traveler* (1832), John Russell had become intrigued with the author's tale of the centuries-old cutlery guilds still operating in Sheffield, England. Russell's company, the Green River Works, evolved into a major supplier of cutlery and tools that would make a profound mark on our nation's development.

John Russell was an innovator. Nearly seventy years before Ford developed his automobile assembly lines, Russell had installed such a mass production system. With his mechanized processes, his plant could produce nearly fifteen times as many knives as the Sheffield guilds Zachariah Allen had written about. Yet Russell suffered a disadvantage: during this era domestically produced items were generally shunned by Americans, who considered European products to be superior. Moreover, when the Sheffield guilds learned that Russell and others, such as Henry Harrington, were competing in their market, they attempted to put the Americans out of business by slashing prices and flooding the American market with their knives.

If not for the Panic of 1837, they might have succeeded. But the Panic put the world economy in such chaos that the Sheffield masters temporarily shelved their plans to undersell the American companies. In the aftermath of the Panic, American knives sold for less than their English counterparts, and the public had incentive to try them. Not only did Russell thus survive the economic turmoil of this period, but his cutlery became a standard of excellence for everything traded in the young nation. From 1835 on, pioneers, trappers, mountain men, and even Indians fighting to save their land relied on Green River knives. Soon anything that was first-rate was said to be "up to the Green River." (In hand-to-hand combat the phrase had a double meaning; if a man could "give it to 'em up to (the) Green River," he could drive the blade of a knife into his opponents as far as the Green River trademark, and was therefore fairly well assured of victory.)

In 1932 the J. Russell and Company Green River Works and the Henry Harrington Company merged to become the present-day Russell Harrington Cutlery Company. Though the business has changed in many ways to maintain a competitive edge, the same care that went into knife making at John Russell's Green River Works is still evident in Russell Harrington's modern manufacturing methods. A forged cook's knife, for example, goes through seventy-two different operations before its completion.

The perfect knife must be manufactured from the finest stain-resistant steel with the appropriate high-carbon content. Russell Harrington uses many types of steel, each of which is analyzed for its hardness, flexibility, and edge-holding characteristics. Because very hard steel is also brittle, each knife is tempered to give it some flexibility. The knife is then further reinforced through *cryogenics*, which involves chilling it at 120 degrees below freezing.

A fine knife must also have the proper shape to its edge. For a perfect edge, all Russell knives are honed by hand, just as they were during the earliest days of the Green River Works. An eighteen-month apprenticeship is required for a worker to learn to hand-grind the hundreds of different tools the company makes.

The heart and soul of Russell Harrington today is Francis Dusza, manager of manufacturing processing. Having entered the company's tool-and-die training program at the age of 16, Dusza has been with Russell Harrington for nearly half a century. Probably the world's foremost living authority on professional cutlery manufacture, he receives numerous requests throughout the year to design or critique knives and tools for special uses.

Dusza offers this advice on the care and feeding of a knife.

A razor-sharp cutting edge has a very fine burr, or "feather," which wavers back and forth with its use. Through repeated use of the knife, the feather begins to "roll over," and the cutting edge dulls. When you stroke the knife on a steel, the feather straightens, returning the cutting edge to its original sharpness. When the feather is so diminished from use that it can no longer be straightened, it is time to return the blade to a sharpening stone. Since competent professional sharpeners are a slowly vanishing breed, you may want to sharpen your knives yourself.

Sharpening stones come in a variety of shapes, sizes and grits. Very practical is a small, rectangular Carborundum stone, with a course grit on one side and a fine grit on the other, sold as a "wet stone" or "oil stone." Any liquid, such as honing oil, water, lemon juice, or liquid soap, will serve as a lubricant.

Just as effective are ceramic stones, which have also come into vogue during recent years. Russell Harrington recently developed a ceramic tri-stone, called the Three-Way Knife Sharpener, which requires no lubrication whatsoever. It is available in restaurant supply stores.

To use any sharpening stone, hold the blade at a sharply acute angle to the stone, roughly fifteen degrees. In other words, lift the back of the blade only a quarter inch or so from the sharpening surface. Then run the blade across the stone in a single direction, flipping it for the reverse stroke. Repeat this procedure several times on the coarse surface, then several times on the fine surface.

Run the blade down a sharpening steel several times, then test the knife by using it. If the edge still isn't sharp enough, repeat the whole procedure to your satisfaction.

Once your knife has a sharp edge, keep it sharp by periodically running it down the shaft of a steel:

Grasp the steel firmly in one hand, placing your thumb securely behind the handle guard. Hold the steel at a comfortable distance, and at a roughly forty-five-degree angle, from your body. With the other hand grasp the handle of the knife.

Rest the heel of the blade against the top of the steel shaft, with the knife and the steel forming an angle slightly greater than 90 degrees. Keeping the cutting edge pressed against the top of the shaft, lift the back of the blade about a quarter of an inch from the steel, forming an angle of 15 to 20 degrees.

Applying constant and moderate pressure, draw the blade smoothly across and down the full length of the steel shaft, until the tip of the knife passes off the steel near the handle guard.

Return the knife to the original position, but this time the blade should rest on the opposite side of the steel.

Test the sharpness of the blade after six passes on each side.

To avoid nicking or needlessly dulling the cutting edge, never toss a knife into a drawer full of other metal utensils. Use a knife rack, or sheathe the blade in plastic. And never wash a knife in an automatic dishwasher, which could not only cause a nicked and dulled edge but could damage the wooden handle.

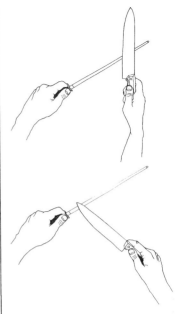

Fine-tuning a cook's knife on a steel. Above: Position to start. Below: Position at finish. Note that the left thumb is securely behind the finger guard.

Avoid leaving a knife immersed in hot, soapy water in a sink. A knife treated this way is unnecessarily exposed to soap and hot water, and there is always the danger of cutting a finger on an unseen sharp edge.

INTRODUCTION

"Every five years, 75 percent of New York City's fourteen thousand restaurants close or change hands," reported *Forbes Magazine* on November 17, 1986. The New York State Restaurant Association confirmed this turnover rate in 1988, when within the five boroughs of metropolitan New York were recorded nineteen thousand restaurants. This statistic reflects the tenuous nature of the restaurant industry. In fact, among all retail industries eating and drinking establishments rank second in their national failure rate (apparel and accessory stores rank first).

Thus it was with great anticipation that I embarked upon this literary venture, preparing manuscript, photographs, and illustrations for a relatively ancient dining establishment. As of the publication of this cookbook, the Pillar House has been in full operation over thirty-six years. Though the current owner's father, George Larsen, could not have known how long the business would last, he did indeed choose a name that reflected its enduring quality. The Pillar House is truly a pillar in today's restaurant industry.

Perhaps the building in which the Pillar House operates has somehow fostered the restaurant's longevity. In my mind I am transported back to the time when Alan Crocker Curtis, an entrepreneur in the paper manufacturing trade, traveled to England on company business. There he first glimpsed the British architecture that inspired the design of his home. Constructed in 1828, the Curtis House faced a road that over a century later ambled only two lanes wide through the sparse suburbs of postwar Boston. That the modern, multilaned 128 opened the same year the Pillar House restaurant opened its doors—after most residential properties adjacent to the road had been purchased by the Commonwealth of Massachusetts and subsequently demolished—confirms a bedrock foundation existed under Curtis's venerable home. I can only surmise the highway was built *around* the 124-year-old building. Could some young civil engineer, in designing the widened highway for modern times, have imagined what the area around Newton and Wellesley must have been like in the early nineteenth century? Could he have felt the presence of a historic landmark, and decided against destruction? Could he have said instead, "We'll build the highway around it"?

Ours is truly a culture of the moment, in which few historic landmarks remain. We are bombarded with instantaneous sensual stimulation, from video and film delivered to our living room to jumbo jet transportation that can take us to almost any corner of the globe in a few hours. Restaurants come and go at a very brisk pace. The Pillar House thus stands out, as a restaurant both in its fourth decade and operating in a structure over a century and a half old.

The Pillar House is special in other ways, including its several rather unorthodox operating policies. First, the restaurant is open Monday through Friday only. Though Saturday is traditionally the busiest day in the restaurant trade, closing on weekends helps to foster a loyal staff, who appreciate the opportunity to spend weekends with their families.

Secondly, smoking of any kind is prohibited inside the restaurant. To implement such a policy in a traditional New England restaurant is risky, but the benefits are multifold. Not only is the dining environment cleaner, it is more in harmony with a high standard of service and cuisine.

And, last, the "back of the house" is open for visits by dining patrons. Though this section of the average commercial restaurant is notoriously poorly maintained, on the Pillar House menu reads this invitation: "Guests are welcome to visit our kitchens." A visit to the back of the house reveals all-weather carpeting, special lighting that is as much like sunlight as possible, and a high level of sanitation, for which all employees are responsible.

Sharing the responsibility for keeping a clean working environment promotes a team spirit among the staff. And teamwork is another ingredient in the Pillar House's tale of success. Further inspection of the kitchen reveals this prominently posted communique:

A THOUGHT FOR EVER
A Little More Teamwork
No Excuses
Concern for the Restaurant
Concern for Your Fellow Worker
Not Just for Yourself, OR *"We're All in This Mess Together"*

This literary endeavor has been most fulfilling and enlightening —from the day when my colleague and longtime friend, chef Alan Gibson, and I first conceived the idea to create a Pillar House cookbook, through all of the ups and downs of the negotiating process, the drafting of the manuscript, and the creation of the photographic plates, to the ultimate release of our cookbook. It is with great pride that we share it with you, our readers and faithful clientele. We wish you great success with all the recipes herein.

DAVID PAUL LAROUSSE

The Essential Pillar House

The secret of great cuisine lies in the raw materials. The finer the quality of the beginning elements, the finer the end product.

The cuisine at the Pillar House can be categorized as American regional with classical influences, a reflection of the restaurant's thirty-six-year evolution. All the elements of this cuisine are made in the traditional manner—from the stocks and the sauces to the breads and the pastries. Pillar House chefs endeavor to purchase only fresh, prime-quality, and preferably locally produced fruits, vegetables, meat, and cheese. And the secret to finding these superior ingredients lies in close and personal contact with the purveyors who supply them.

One of the tasks of the executive chef at the Pillar House is an occasional excursion through the primary commercial markets in and around metropolitan Boston: the New England produce center in Chelsea, the fish pier in South Boston, the meat center at Newmarket Square. An early-morning expedition through these vibrant commercial centers not only affords the chef personal contact with his purveyors; it also sparks his culinary creativity. Walking through one hundred yards of high-piled crates of fresh produce, or watching fishermen unload six tons of fish from a deep-sea vessel, allows ideas to flow. Here begins the preparation for a day's epicurean specialties.

When not perusing the early-morning markets, the chef generally begins his work day at 9:00 A.M. He makes a full tour of the restaurant, inspecting all areas and greeting the members of the day staff. He meets with the purchasing steward, the sous-chef, and the pastry chef to discuss the day's featured dishes.

At 11:30 the lunch service begins. The chef oversees production and lends a hand where required. When the lunch service is ended, he meets with the evening staff, and once again reviews the dinner features. At these meetings he also considers customers' special requests, such as a dish that meets dietary restrictions or an item not listed on the printed menu. The staff takes considerable pride in being willing and able to prepare any special dish a patron might wish for.

The chef then meets with the beverage director, who doubles as wine purchasing agent. They discuss upcoming dinner banquets and consider the appropriate wines to accompany each course. For each of the past eight years, the *Wine Spectator*, the *Wall Street Journal* of the American wine community, has designated the Pillar House one of the one hundred U.S. dining establishments offering an outstanding wine list.

As the dinner service begins, the chef tastes sauces and soups, inspects various stations throughout the kitchen, and in general makes sure that the evening's production will be smooth and successful. Throughout the evening he continues touring the back of the house, answering questions and often joining the main cooking line. At once he must be cook, manager, menu composer, and problem solver. Even when the dinner service winds down he can't go home; instead he heads for his office to phone in orders to purveyors, tackle some paperwork, and jot down reminders for the next day. As Anton Mosimann, executive chef at the celebrated Dorchester Hotel in London, once admonished me, "A really good cuisine demands a single-minded, almost holy devotion."

Cooking for other people touches them in profound ways. Good home cooking can be not only satisfying but exciting—as exciting as a fine restaurant meal. To make it this way, the home cook may need to master some professional methods. We've therefore included detailed explanations of techniques, notes on tricks of the trade, and a glossary. These will allow you to successfully replicate Pillar House dishes, rather than just reminisce about them.

Precise measuring is sometimes essential, particularly in baking. Since weighing is often more exact than measuring by volume, quantities of certain ingredients are specified by weight. Note that the volume equivalent, given in parentheses for flour, is approximate. (For butter, just remember that 1 ounce equals 2 tablespoons.)

Fresh ingredients, of course, give best results. Even herbs should be used in their fresh state when possible, since drying destroys some of their flavor. Unless dried herbs are specified, amounts given are for the fresh version.

Spices, likewise, should be fresh-ground. A small nutmeg grater is indispensable for releasing the pungent aroma and flavor of that spice. For grinding other spices, such as clove, allspice, cumin, dill seed, and coriander seed, a mortar and pestle are recommended.

Except where indicated, each recipe serves four.

ALAN R. GIBSON, CEC/CCE

Glossary

Although it is impossible to teach everything we know about cooking in a single volume, we are nevertheless wholeheartedly dedicated to sharing the techniques employed at the Pillar House, without withholding any secrets. We have therefore included this section on culinary basics. To create a foundation from which to work, less experienced cooks should familiarize themselves thoroughly with the definitions included here.

AL DENTE: Literally, "to the tooth" or "to the bite." This term is used in reference to pasta and vegetables cooked till tender but not mushy, so they are still somewhat firm and resilient when bitten.

BLANCH: To place a food in boiling salted water, stock, court bouillon, or another liquid to partially cook it, set its color, or facilitate peeling.

BOIL: To cook a food in water or another liquid at 212° F. A full rolling boil is essential for cooking some foods (such as pasta), but undesirable for cooking others (such as stocks).

CARAMELIZE: To cook sugar or another food in a sauté or sauce pan over direct heat long enough to allow the sugar, or the sugar in the food, to begin to brown. Caramelizing imparts a brown color and a nutty flavor to the finished dish. (See the recipes for *demi-glace* and Praline and Peach Cheesecake.)

CELLOPHANE NOODLES: An Asian pasta made from bean flour. Cook these noodles as any other pasta—drop them into boiling water and simmer until al dente. The noodles cook fairly rapidly, in 1 to 2 minutes.

DE-BEARD: To remove the fibrous strands extending from the side of a fresh mussel. It is by these strands that a mussel attaches and holds itself to shoreline rocks.

DICE: To cut foods into small cubes. Generally, small dice is ⅛ inch square, medium dice is ¼ inch square, and large dice is ⅜ to ½ inch square.

DOCK: To pierce raw pastry with the tines of a fork. Steam is produced inside the pastry when the butter melts; docking allows this steam to escape, preventing the dough from rising too much.

EGG WASH: Beaten whole egg, sometimes with water or milk added, brushed onto a pastry exterior. When the pastry is baked the egg browns slightly, resulting in a glossy, golden-brown appearance.

EMULSION: A liquid slightly thickened by the suspension of minute drops of oil or fat, for example, hollandaise sauce or vinaigrette.

FOLD: Using a rubber spatula, to gently combine two food components, one being highly whipped. This allows the whipped product to retain its whipped-in air. The technique is used in such dishes as soufflé and dessert mousse.

FOOD MILL: With the advent of food processors for both the home and professional markets, this marvelously simple gadget has fallen on hard times. But in puréeing soups and sauces it can be a tremendous aid. It consists of a straight-sided container with a perforated bottom. In a hole in the center rests the shaft, bent out and up at 90° angles, with a nob attached to the top end. A curved flange attached to the shaft presses against the perforated bottom. To operate the mill, you pour a soup or sauce into the container and turn the crank. The soup or sauce is puréed as its solids are pressed through the perforated bottom. (See *Sieve*.)

GANACHE: A mixture of cooked chocolate, cream, and flavorings. A pastry chef's staple, it is used as both a filling and a confectionary coating, or icing. Of commonly known confections, chocolate truffles most closely resemble this mixture.

JULIENNE: Any food cut into strips, from ⅛ by ⅛ by 1 inch to ¼ by ¼ by 2 or 3 inches. To cut into such a strip.

MINCE: To chop an herb or vegetable very fine.

Above: *A carrot cut into three julienne sizes, with rectangular slices at right.* Below: *Small, medium, and large dice, with small julienne at right.*

MONTÉE: From the French verb *monter*, "to lift," this term means to incorporate butter into a sauce or soup just before it is served. By stirring in the butter in small pieces, you create an emulsion, slightly thickening the sauce or soup. The flavor of the final product is thus improved, or lifted.

PARISIENNE SCOOP: Commonly known as a melon baller, this tool creates spherical garnishes from fruits and vegetables.

POACH: To cook gently in simmering liquid, at 190° to 200° F. (See the recipe for Poached Filet of Salmon, Lemon Thyme Sauce.)

REDUCE: To simmer or boil a sauce or stock to decrease its volume, through evaporation, and to increase its flavor and thickness.

RENDER: To liquidize bacon, fatback, chicken fat, or other fat by cooking it in a heavy-gauge pan over medium heat.

SAFFRON: The dried, orange stigmas of a variety of purple-flowering crocus. A native of southern Europe, this flower is cultivated in England, France, Spain, Turkey, Greece, Persia, Kashmir, and China. Saffron is indispensable in dishes such as French bouillabaisse and Spanish paella. It is very expensive because the stigmas must be hand-picked at dawn, the moment the flower opens, during a two-week harvest season. Each flower, moreover, holds only three stigmas; two hundred thousand stigmas are required to produce 1 pound of saffron. But a small amount of saffron yields much aroma and color. Saffron is available, in the form of tiny strands, in fractions of a gram. In this book it is called for in pinches; ¼ gram yields three pinches.

SAUCE PAN: A heavy-gauge round cooking vessel with vertical sides and a single handle.

SAUTÉ: From the French verb *sauter*, "to jump." To cook food in a small amount of fat or oil.

SAUTÉ PAN: A round cooking vessel with sloping sides and a single handle.

SIEVE: A fine-screened strainer through which sauces and other foods are pressed, usually with the help of a rubber spatula. Pastry cream is pressed through a sieve to remove any lumps; raspberry purée is pressed through to remove the raspberry seeds. A food mill serves the same purpose.

SKILLET: Generally, a heavy-gauge cast-iron pan with a single handle. Sometimes called a Griswold pan, it can be placed in the oven, thus doubling as a roasting pan.

WHITE PEPPER: Black pepper with its hull removed. Because of its light color, ground white pepper is preferred over black for certain light-colored sauces and dishes. You may prefer, however, to see the dark specs of black pepper. We recommend keeping two pepper mills, one for black, one for white, and labeling each accordingly.

ZEST: The outer, pigmented skin of lemons, limes, grapefruits, and oranges. The oils in the zest give a dish a pungent aroma of citrus. To remove the zest from citrus fruits, use a zester, a small, five-holed skinning tool; or shave off strips with a vegetable peeler and chop the strips into thin slivers.

Chef Alan Gibson works the line with brigade member Douglas Steward.

Feel free to substitute any fresh ripe fruit of your preference, such as pineapple, blackberries, kiwis, apples, pears, mango, and papaya.

1 • Starters

COLD APPETIZERS

Chilled Seasonal Fruits with Sorbet

4 ½-inch wedges cantaloupe, seeded and skinned
4 ½-inch wedges, honeydew melon, seeded and skinned
8 strawberries
½ pint raspberries
½ star fruit (carambola), cut into 4 slices
½ bunch red seedless grapes
½ bunch Thompson seedless grapes
4 scoops sorbet
1 bunch mint

♦ Trim the strawberry tops, then gently rinse the fruit. Gently rinse the raspberries. Rinse the grapes, and, with scissors, snip them into smaller bunches. Rinse and dry the mint. Chill all the fruit.
♦ Arrange the fruit on four chilled plates. Place a scoop of your choice of sorbets (pages 105–6) in the center of each arrangement. Garnish with fresh mint, and serve.

Irish Smoked Salmon, Classical Presentation

(MAPLE-MUSTARD SAUCE)
3 tablespoons mustard seed
2 tablespoons dry mustard
1½ teaspoons turmeric
1 teaspoon fresh tarragon leaves
¼ cup white wine vinegar
3 tablespoons olive oil
1 teaspoon minced garlic
¼ cup medium dark amber maple syrup

(TO ASSEMBLE)

6 slices toasted Anadama bread (page 74) or other bread

4 3-ounce portions Irish smoked salmon

4 leaves bibb lettuce, washed and dried

4 leaves radicchio, washed and dried

12 leaves belgian endive, washed and dried

4 teaspoons hard-cooked egg whites, sieved

4 teaspoons hard-cooked egg yolks, sieved

4 teaspoons small-diced red bermuda onion

4 teaspoons capers, drained

2 teaspoons grated carrot

maple-mustard sauce

To hard-cook eggs, place them in a sauce pan, and cover them with cold tap water. Add 1 tablespoon salt per four eggs. Bring the water to a boil, and continue boiling for exactly 10 minutes. Remove the pan from the fire, drain the eggs, and immediately immerse them in cold water. Continue adding cold water until the eggs have fully cooled. Gently crack and remove the shells. Keep the eggs immersed in cold water until you are ready to use them.

(MAPLE-MUSTARD SAUCE)

♦ Combine the mustard seed, dry mustard, turmeric, tarragon, vinegar, and olive oil. Bring the mixture to a boil, remove it from the fire, and let it sit overnight. The next day add the maple syrup, and purée all in a food processor. Set the sauce aside.

(TO ASSEMBLE)

♦ Trim the crusts from all four slices of the toast, then cut each slice diagonally in both directions, producing sixteen triangular "points."

♦ On chilled plates, arrange the slices of smoked salmon down the center. On one side of this line of salmon, arrange a line of four toast points. On the other side of the salmon place one leaf each of the lettuce, endive, and radicchio. Place the remaining garnish—egg whites and yolks, red onion, capers, and grated carrot—on the leaves. Serve the sauce separately, or ladle it over the center of the salmon.

Wine recommendation: 1985 Wehlener Sonnenuhr Riesling Kabinet (Germany)

Oysters and Littlenecks on the Half Shell

(COCKTAIL SAUCE)

1 medium onion, cut into eighths

1 small clove garlic

5 tablespoons frozen apple juice concentrate

¾ cup tomato paste

½ cup malt vinegar

½ teaspoon cayenne pepper

¼ teaspoon ground cinnamon

⅛ teaspoon ground cloves

2 teaspoons Worcestershire sauce

2 tablespoons prepared horseradish

To open clams and oysters, first scrub their exteriors in cold water with a stiff brush.

Grasp each clam, one at a time, in the palm of your hand, with the hinged side resting on the fleshy part of the palm underneath the thumb. Hold the cutting edge of a clam knife at the slit where the two shells meet. Wrap the fingers of the hand holding the clam around the knife, and squeeze until the knife slides between the shells. Push the knife up into the clam, scraping along the inside of the top shell. Avoid cutting through the center of the clam, which would tear the flesh. Pull off the top shell and discard it. Slide the knife underneath the flesh to loosen it from the bottom shell.

Place each oyster, one at a time, on a clean cloth over a hard work surface. Hold the oyster firmly in place with one hand. With the other hand, press the point of the oyster knife into the small opening at the pointed end of the oyster. Press the knife downward to lift the top shell. When it pops, it has separated from the inner flesh. Scrape the underside of the top shell, then lift it off. Run the knife underneath the oyster meat to loosen it from the bottom shell.

(RASPBERRY MIGNONETTE SAUCE)
1 cup raspberry vinegar
¼ cup dry white wine
1 teaspoon coarse-ground pepper
1 teaspoon salt
1 shallot, minced
1 teaspoon minced fresh basil leaves

(REMOULADE SAUCE)
2 egg yolks
2 tablespoons dijon mustard
pinch each of salt and white pepper
4 teaspoons chopped parsley
1 anchovy filet, mashed
1 cup olive oil
¼ cup white wine vinegar
1 tablespoon capers, drained
¼ cup small-diced gherkins

(TO SERVE)
the sauces
crushed ice
12 littleneck clams
12 oysters
1 large lemon, cut into 8 wedges
4 sprigs parsley

♦ Prepare the sauces at least twenty-four hours in advance to allow their ingredients to marry.

(COCKTAIL SAUCE)
♦ Purée all of the ingredients in a food processor. Place the sauce in a small container, cover it, and chill.

(RASPBERRY MIGNONETTE SAUCE)
♦ Combine all the ingredients. Cover the sauce, and chill it.

(REMOULADE SAUCE)
♦ Put the yolks, mustard, salt, pepper, parsley, and anchovy into a food processor. Turn the machine on. Add the olive oil, in a slow, steady stream, alternately with the vinegar. Continue until all the olive oil and vinegar has been added and a thick, emulsified sauce results. Stir in the capers and diced gherkins.

(TO SERVE)
♦ Take twelve small ramekins (oyster cups), and fill four with one sauce, four with another, and four with the third. Place one ramekin of each sauce in the center of each of four dinner plates. Arrange a layer of crushed ice over the plate, around the three sauces. Arrange three oysters and three clams on the bed of ice. Garnish each plate with two lemon wedges and a sprig of fresh parsley.

Wine recommendation: Domaine Chandon Sparkling Brut (California)

Chilled Gulf Shrimp Cocktail

1 onion, cut into eighths
1 bay leaf
½ teaspoon peppercorns,
    crushed
1 bunch parsley stems

1 lemon, peeled and quartered
1 tablespoon salt
20 16/20-count raw shrimp, in
    their shells

- Add the first six ingredients to a gallon of water, and bring it to a boil. Simmer for 15 minutes.
- Peel and devein the shrimp, leaving the last section of the tail intact.
- Drop the shrimp into the boiling water. Leave the pot on the fire for 3 minutes.
- Remove the pot from the fire and check that the shrimp is done. Then drain the shrimp, and place it in ice water.
- To serve the shrimp, remove it from the water and pat it dry. Serve five per person, with one of the three sauces on pages 7–8.

Lobster and Scallop Mousse, Sweet Red Pepper Purée

(MOUSSE, PART I)
1 tablespoon butter
1 teaspoon shallots, minced
8 ounces (1 cup) scallops
2 tablespoons dry white wine

1 tablespoon lemon juice
pinch each of salt and white
    pepper

(MOUSSE, PART II)
1 slice fresh white bread,
    trimmed of crust
7 ounces (1 cup) cooked
    lobster meat
3 tablespoons lemon juice
1 egg white

3 tablespoons dry white wine
the cooked scallops and wine
    reduction
4 teaspoons butter
pinch nutmeg
1 cup heavy cream

(RED PEPPER PURÉE)
3 large, unblemished red bell
    peppers
2 egg yolks
½ shallot, minced
¼ cup minced fresh basil
    leaves

salt and white pepper
3–4 drops Tabasco sauce
1 cup olive oil
juice of 1 small lemon

(TO SERVE)
1 each: red, green, and yellow
    bell pepper
radicchio

butter lettuce
belgian endive

16/20-count *means the shrimp number sixteen to twenty per pound. 16/20s are smaller than U-12s, which number under twelve per pound. The smallest shrimp,* titi, *are sold shelled and precooked.*

One of the worst, and sadly most common, gastronomic faux pas is the overcooking of fish, particularly shellfish. Like lobster and scallops, shrimp should be cooked just until they lose their translucence. In the case of shrimp, this requires only a few minutes. Overcooked shellfish is dry and rubbery.

Deveining shrimp is simple. Once the shell is removed, run the blade of a sharp paring knife down the back of the shrimp, scoring about ⅛ inch into the flesh. Under running cold water, rinse out any impurities that lie in this channel.

You can also roast peppers by impaling them on a fork, one at a time, and holding them over an open gas flame; turn occasionally until the skin blackens. Or place the peppers under the gas flame of a broiler and, again, turn occasionally until the skin blackens and bubbles away from the flesh. Our technique is as effective as these two alternatives, however, and is considerably less laborious.

To shape the mousse into ovals, scoop approximately ¼ cup, with a tablespoon, into the palm of one hand, the hand slightly moistened with cold water. Turn the mousse several times in your cupped palm, using the tablespoon to shape it into an oval. Serve 2 or 3 ovals per person.

(MOUSSE, PART I)

◆ Sauté the shallots in butter about 3 minutes. Add the scallops, and sauté 30 seconds. Remove the scallops with a slotted spoon, and set them aside. Add the white wine, lemon juice, salt, and white pepper to the pan, and reduce by half.

(MOUSSE, PART II)

◆ Put the bread slice into a food processor, and turn the machine on for 3 or 4 seconds, until the bread is reduced to crumbs. Add the lobster and 2 tablespoons lemon juice, and blend all together.
◆ Add the egg white, the white wine, 1 tablespoon lemon juice, the cooked scallops, and the wine reduction, and blend again. Add the butter and nutmeg, and purée once more.
◆ Add the cream, and blend for 4 seconds, just until it is incorporated.
◆ Transfer this mixture to a well-buttered soufflé mold, ramekin, or other suitable dish. Cover tightly with plastic wrap, and refrigerate a minimum of 3 hours.

(RED PEPPER PURÉE)

◆ Place the peppers on a roasting pan in a preheated 400° F oven, and roast them until their skins begin to turn black.
◆ Remove the peppers from the oven, place them in a plastic bag, and seal the bag. After 10 minutes take the peppers from the bag, tear them open, and remove the seeds and interior ribbing. Tear the skin from the flesh, scraping with a paring knife where necessary. Pat the flesh dry, and discard the seeds and skin.
◆ Put the egg yolks, shallot, basil, salt, pepper, and Tabasco into the food processor. Turn it on, and pour in the olive oil in a slow, steady stream, alternately with the lemon juice. Continue until all the olive oil and lemon juice is incorporated and an emulsified sauce results. Add the roasted peppers, and purée. Thin the sauce with dry white wine if necessary.

(TO SERVE)

◆ Dip the mold into very hot water for 5 seconds. Invert it onto a serving platter, and remove it. If the mousse will not slip out of its mold on the first try, dip it into the hot water for another 5 seconds and try again.
◆ Serve the mousse sliced or shaped into ovals on individual plates, over the sauce.
◆ Dice the peppers very small, and sprinkle them over the top of each serving of mousse. Place leaves of radicchio, butter lettuce, and belgian endive to one side.

Wine recommendation: Pedro Domeco Dry Sherry (Spain)

Arkansas Razorback Pâté, Chef's Presentation

⅛ teaspoon each of ground allspice, nutmeg, basil, marjoram, paprika, rosemary, and thyme
1 bay leaf
3 white peppercorns
2 pounds boneless shoulder of wild boar, trimmed of excess fat and cut into ½-inch strips
juice and zest of 1 orange
¼ cup sliced onion
2 cloves garlic, minced

6 juniper berries
2 whole cloves
½ cup dry red wine
1 pound salt pork, trimmed of rind and cut into ½-inch strips
1 cup fresh white bread crumbs
½ cup pistachio nuts, quartered
¾ pound medium-diced bacon
16 strips bacon

- In a blender, electric spice blender, or mortar with pestle, blend the herbs and spices, bay leaf, and peppercorns. (If you do not possess any of these tools, purchase the herbs and spices in their powdered form.)
- Combine the meat, herb-spice mixture, orange zest and juice, onion, garlic, juniper berries, cloves, and wine. Marinate in the refrigerator for 24 hours, then drain off the liquid and discard the berries and cloves.
- Place a meat grinder or meat grinding attachment to a food processor in the freezer for 20 minutes.
- Grind the boar shoulder, salt pork, and onions twice—once through a large-holed grinding plate, and once through a fine-holed plate.
- In a bowl, blend the ground meat with the bread crumbs, pistachios, and diced bacon.
- Preheat an oven to 275°F.
- Line a 2-quart pâté mold or other suitable metal mold with the bacon strips, which should hang over the side.
- Fill the lined mold with the pâté mixture, press it down gently, and flip the ends of the bacon strips over. The top of the pâté should be completely covered with bacon.
- Place the mold in a roasting pan, fill the pan halfway with hot water, and bake at 275°F for 1½ hours.
- Take the pâté from the oven, and allow it to cool. Then remove it from the mold, cover it, and refrigerate it. Serve it garnished with marinated mushrooms (pages 31–32) and cornichons (pickled baby gherkins).

Wine recommendation: 1986 Les Chazelles Mâcon-Villages (France)

This recipe was originally created with Razorback boar, a variety of wild pig found in Arkansas. Hence the name of the dish.

Wild boar, when sold in a butcher shop, must have been inspected and shown to meet federal sanitation requirements. If you have an aversion to cooking wild meat, substitute a boneless shoulder of domestic pork.

Though others in your household may conclude you have flipped your gastronomic lid when you place a meat grinder in the freezer, this step is important. Chilling the grinder helps to keep the meat and fat firm, thus allowing a cleaner and sharper grind.

Pâtés (along with terrines, quenelles, and savory mousses) belong to a group of culinary preparations known as farces, *from the French verb* farcir, *"to stuff." Farce also means a "practical joke," or a "prank." This is because it was once common to play a joke on one's guests by filling a hen, fish, or some other small animal with a* farce.

Button mushrooms, also know as Paris or Parisienne mushrooms, are the smallest size of the off-white, round-top mushrooms available in most markets year-round. Chanterelles and morels, both wild varieties, have been cultivated by a number of enterprising farmers the past few years. Shitake is a Japanese variety, also cultivated. If chanterelles, morels, or shitakes are unavailable fresh, we suggest substituting dried. Canned mushrooms are much less desirable, since they are packed in water and have thus lost most of their flavor. You can also substitute other mushroom varieties.

Crème fraiche, the French version of sour cream, has a higher fat content. Refrigerated, it will keep up to thirty days. Use it as you would sour cream. You can also work it into salad dressings, savory sauces, and dessert sauces.

Sometimes the fat in homemade crème fraiche will rise to the top, leaving the excess liquid below. You should therefore remove what you need from the top of the bowl, and avoid stirring or shaking up the remainder. As you work your way closer to the watery part, you may wish to discard it.

A commercial crème fraiche can now be found in some American supermarkets. You can also substitute regular sour cream, or, if you are really fat-conscious, plain low-fat yoghurt. If you use yoghurt, however, avoid overcooking it after adding it to the mushroom mixture. Because it has so little fat, when boiled it will curdle.

HOT APPETIZERS

A Quartet of Mushrooms in Pastry

(CRÈME FRAICHE)
2 cups heavy cream
½ teaspoon salt

2 cups sour cream

(CROUSTADES AND FILLING)
½ cup fresh chanterelle mushrooms
½ cup fresh morel mushrooms
½ cup fresh shitake mushrooms
½ cup fresh button mushrooms
juice of 1 lemon
1 pound puff pastry dough (pages 87–88)

1 egg, beaten
2 tablespoons olive oil
1 tablespoon minced garlic
¼ teaspoon minced fresh thyme leaves
¼ teaspoon minced fresh oregano
½ cup *crème fraiche*
salt and white pepper to taste

(CRÈME FRAICHE)
♦ Blend the ingredients in a saucepan.
♦ Slowly heat the mixture on medium heat to 100°F.
♦ Remove from heat and refrigerate for at least eight hours.

(CROUSTADES AND FILLING)
♦ Preheat an oven to 375°F.
♦ Gently rinse the four varieties of mushrooms in cold water and the juice of one lemon. Wrap them in paper towels, and set them aside to dry. (To avoid splattering, they must be completely dry before you add them to the hot olive oil.)
♦ On a lightly floured board or counter top, roll out the puff pastry dough into a rectangle about ⅛-inch thick. Cut this into eight smaller rectangles, each approximately 3 by 4 inches. Lightly brush four of these rectangles with the beaten egg. Place one of the other four rectangles on top of each of the egg-washed rectangles. Brush off excess flour. Transfer the double rectangles to a lightly buttered baking sheet, and brush the top of each with beaten egg. Bake the rectangles 15 to 20 minutes, or until they are golden brown.
♦ Remove the sheet from the oven, and set it aside. (Any excess puff pastry dough can be wrapped in plastic and used later.)
♦ In a sauté pan, heat the olive oil until it just begins to smoke. Add the mushrooms, and sauté them briefly. Add the herbs and garlic, and toss all the ingredients together. Add the *crème fraiche*, bring to a simmer, then remove the pan from the fire.

- Split each puff pastry *croustade* in half horizontally. Fill the bottom half with the mushroom mixture, then place the other half on top, and serve.

Baked Brie with Brown Sugar Almonds

½ cup sliced almonds
1 tablespoon brown sugar
4 tablespoons apricot jam

2 4-ounce rounds of brie cheese, cut in half crosswise to make four thinner rounds

- Preheat an oven to 400°F.
- Combine the almonds, brown sugar, and apricot jam in a bowl, and blend. Divide this mixture into four equal portions.
- Place the brie halves, cut side up, on a baking sheet. Top each round with a portion of the almond, jam, and sugar mixture. Bake 8 minutes.
- Remove the rounds, and serve them hot with toasted Anadama bread (page 74).

Salmon Tortellini in Vodka Cream

(SALMON MOUSSE)
1 shallot, minced
1 ounce butter
½ cup boned and skinned salmon filet cut into 1-inch cubes
2 pinches each of salt and white pepper

1 teaspoon minced fresh dill
4 tablespoons dry white wine
pinch nutmeg
2 large egg yolks
6 tablespoons heavy cream

(TORTELLINI)
2 cups unbleached white flour
3 large eggs
1 teaspoon olive oil

pinch salt
1 tablespoon minced fresh dill
salmon mousse

(TO COOK THE TORTELLINI)
1 tablespoon salt
2 tablespoons olive oil

the raw tortellini
1 ounce butter

(VODKA CREAM SAUCE)
1 shallot, minced
1 teaspoon minced garlic
1 ounce butter
2 tablespoons vodka

2 teaspoons dijon mustard
1 cup *crème fraiche* (page 12) or sour cream

If you can't find the time for making your own tortellini, substitute 1 pound of any variety available in your local market. Sauté the salmon and the dill in the sauce instead.

If you dislike the tedious chore of mincing garlic with a knife, employ a good garlic press. It will instantly purée the powerful stuff, one clove at a time. Or, if you are a true garlic aficionado and use a lot of it, peel two, three, or more bulbs, put the peeled cloves into a food processor, add a bit of olive oil, and purée all. Covered tight and stored in the refrigerator, the purée will keep its potency for a good two weeks. (This technique can also be employed with shallots.)

(TO ASSEMBLE)

the cooked tortellini   salt and white pepper

the sauce

(SALMON MOUSSE)

- Sauté the shallot in the butter for 1 minute. Add the salmon, salt, pepper, and dill. Sauté 4 minutes.
- Add the wine and simmer for 2 minutes. Remove from the fire and let cool 10 minutes.
- Purée the mixture in a food processor. Add the nutmeg, egg yolk, and cream. Purée just until smooth; do not overwork. Set the mixture aside.

(TORTELLINI)

- Sift the flour into a large mixing bowl. Make a well in the center. Add the eggs, olive oil, salt, and dill. Blend all together until the dough comes away from the side of the bowl.
- Place the dough on a well-floured surface, and knead at least 10 minutes, until the dough is shiny, smooth, and elastic. Wrap it in plastic, and refrigerate it for 30 minutes.
- Roll out the pasta dough very thin, approximately $1/32$-inch thick, on a floured board. Cut out 2-inch circles.
- Place approximately $1/4$ teaspoon of the salmon mousse in the center of each circle. Brush the edge of the circle lightly with water. Fold each circle in half, and press the edges together to seal them. Lift one of the corners up and turn it in to the center of the folded edge. Moisten the remaining corner, fold it over, and press it onto the opposite corner. Press the corners together to seal them. Repeat this procedure until all the salmon mousse or all the dough is used up.

(TO COOK THE TORTELLINI)

- In a large pot, add the salt and olive oil to $1\frac{1}{2}$ gallons water. Bring the water to a rapid boil. Add the tortellini, bring the water to a boil again, and cook until the pasta is al dente. Drain the tortellini, then stir in the butter. Set the tortellini aside.

(VODKA CREAM SAUCE)

- Sauté the shallot and garlic in the butter for 3 minutes. Add the vodka and the mustard, and stir to blend. Add the *crème fraiche*, stir to blend, and bring to a boil.

(TO ASSEMBLE)

- Add the tortellini to the sauce, and season to taste with salt and pepper. Toss and serve.

Snails with Burgundy Wine and Garlic

24 large snails
3 tablespoons minced garlic
1 shallot, minced
1 ounce butter

1 cup dry red wine
½ pound unsalted butter
12 red-skinned potatoes

- ◆ Thoroughly rinse the snails in cold water. Drain them, pat them dry, and set them aside.
- ◆ Sauté the garlic and shallots in the butter. Add the red wine, and reduce by a third. Add the snails.
- ◆ Cut the butter into ½-inch cubes. Add them to the wine mixture, and stir continuously until the butter is completely incorporated. Remove the mixture from the fire, and set it aside.
- ◆ Preheat an oven to 375°F.
- ◆ Cut the potatoes in half, and scoop out the center of each with a parisienne scoop, or melon baller (save the scooped out part for another dish). Place these potato *socles* in boiling salted water, and boil them until they are tender but still firm (about 5 minutes). *Do not overcook them.*
- ◆ Place the potato *socles* in an *escargotiere*. Place a snail in each *socle*, and fill with some of the sauce.
- ◆ Bake the snails and potatoes 30 minutes. Serve them immediately, with extra, heated sauce poured over, and hot french bread.

Wine recommendation: 1982 Acacia Pinot Noir (California)

Warm Sea Scallops, Dijon Cream

(POTATO BORDER)
2 cups Pillar House Whipped
    Potatoes (page 70)

3 egg yolks
salt and white pepper

(SCALLOPS)
1½ cups sea scallops
3 tablespoons butter
¼ cup dry white wine
1 cup *crème fraiche* (page 12)

3 teaspoons dijon mustard
pinch fresh thyme
salt and white pepper

(POTATO BORDER)
- ◆ Prepare "duchess potatoes": Stir the three yolks into the mashed potatoes, and blend well. Season to taste with salt and pepper.
- ◆ Preheat an oven to 375°F.
- ◆ Fill a pastry bag, fitted with a #9 star tip, with the mashed potatoes. Pipe a border onto the edges of four coquilles or four small casserole dishes. Bake 8 to 10 minutes, or until the potatoes are golden brown.

To remove the smell of garlic from your hands, rinse them with fresh lemon juice.

   If you doubt the medicinal and health-giving properties of garlic, remember this saying: "Garlic is as good as ten mothers."

An escargotiere *is a small stainless steel or ceramic dish with half a dozen round indentations in the bottom. These hold the snail shells or, in this case, the potato socles in place. If you haven't such a dish, remove a small slice from the bottom of each potato half before cooking and place the* socles *in an ordinary casserole dish or baking pan.*

The little ball scooped out of the center of each potato half can be stored in the refrigerator, immersed in cold water. Deep fried, or sautéed in butter and herbs, these make an excellent side dish.

How to Use a Pastry Bag

Drop the pastry tip into the open bag so the tip extends out from the smaller end. (You may need to trim the smaller end of the bag with scissors, an eighth of an inch at a time, until it fits snugly.)

Fold the larger end of the bag over, forming a collar 3 to 4 inches wide. Grasp the bag with one hand, underneath the collar. With the opposing hand, using a rubber spatula, fill the pastry bag with the mashed potatoes, whipped cream, dessert mousse, or whatever else you will be piping out.

With both hands, grasp the collar and flip it back up. Gently shake the bag so the ingredients slide down toward the tip. Gather the bag around the ingredients, and gently twist it closed. Squeeze the bag gently, starting a flow of the ingredients.

With one hand grasping the twisted end of the bag and the other hand guiding the tip, gently squeeze until the ingredients flow out. Control the flow of food from the tip with pressure from both hands. When the bag is nearly empty, refill it and continue piping.

Remove any remaining food from the bag and save it for some other use. Remove the tip, and immediately wash both it and the bag with warm soapy water. Refold the collar, and stand the bag in a dish drainer on absorbent paper until it dries completely.

(SCALLOPS)
- Sauté the scallops in the butter for 3 minutes. Remove them with a slotted spoon, and set them aside. Add the white wine to the butter, and reduce by half. Add the remaining ingredients: *crème fraiche*, mustard, thyme, and salt and pepper to taste. Add the scallops, and bring the mixture to a simmer.
- Carefully spoon the scallop mixture into the coquilles or casseroles.

Cape Scallops, Saffron Sauce

(SAFFRON SAUCE)

3 ounces butter	1 cup heavy cream
1 shallot, minced	2 ounces butter
¼ cup dry white wine	salt and white pepper
2 pinches saffron	

(SCALLOPS)

24 ounces sea scallops	1 ounce butter

(VEGETABLES)

4 baby carrots, with tops on	1 ounce butter
4 baby white eggplants	salt and white pepper
4 baby patty pan squashes	

(TO ASSEMBLE)

the scallop-sauce mixture	the vegetables

(SAFFRON SAUCE)
- Sauté the shallot in 1 ounce butter for 3 minutes. Add the wine, and reduce by half.
- Add the saffron, and toss briefly. Add the heavy cream, and reduce by half.
- *Montée* 2 ounces butter: add it in small pieces, stirring until it is fully incorporated. Season the sauce to taste with salt and pepper. Set it aside.

(SCALLOPS)
- In a separate pan, sauté the scallops in 1 ounce butter for five minutes. Add the scallops to the sauce.

(VEGETABLES)
- In boiling, salted water, blanch the baby vegetables until they are al dente.
- Sauté the vegetables in 1 ounce butter, and season them to taste with salt and pepper.

(TO ASSEMBLE)

♦ Bring the scallop mixture to a boil, then spoon it into an appropriate serving dish. Garnish with the baby vegetables.

Wine recommendation: 1986 Duckhorn Sauvignon Blanc (California)

If the baby vegetables listed are unavailable, substitute others, or cut "grown-up" vegetables into slices, julienne sticks, or parisienne balls.

Poached Salmon Marseillaise

(TO POACH)

½ ounce butter
4 3-ounce boned and skinned
    salmon filets
½ cup fennel root, julienned
¼ cup carrot, julienned
¼ cup celery, julienned
¼ cup leek, white part only,
    julienned
2 medium tomatoes, peeled,
    seeded, and medium-diced
    (tomato fondue, page 19)

8 fresh mussels, in the shell,
    de-bearded and well
    scrubbed
pinch each of salt and white
    pepper
¼ cup dry white wine
2 tablespoons Pernod
½ teaspoon minced garlic

(SAUCE)

1 shallot, minced
1 ounce butter
¼ cup dry white wine
2 pinches saffron

1 cup heavy cream
1 ounce butter
salt and white pepper

(TO ASSEMBLE)

the poached salmon,
    vegetables, and mussels

the sauce

(TO POACH)

♦ Preheat an oven to 375°F. Butter a small baking dish, and place the four salmon filets in it. Top them with the julienned vegetables, tomatoes, mussels, garlic, salt, pepper, white wine, Pernod, and garlic.
♦ Cover the dish with aluminum foil, place the dish in the oven, and bake for 10 to 15 minutes. Remove the dish from the oven.
♦ Lift open one corner of the foil, and very carefully pour out the juices for later use. Recover the baking dish, and set it aside in a warm place.

(SAUCE)

♦ Sauté the shallot in the butter. Add the white wine, and reduce until almost (but not quite) dry. Add the reserved juices and the saffron, and reduce by two-thirds. Add the cream, and reduce again by half. *Montée* the butter until it is fully incorporated. Season to taste with salt and pepper.

(TO ASSEMBLE)
◆ Place the salmon filets on individual plates or on an appropriate serving platter. Top each filet with a portion of the julienned vegetables, mussels, and tomatoes. Ladle some sauce over, and serve.

Sautéed Mussels with Fennel and Saffron Fettuccine

(PASTA DOUGH)

2 cups unbleached white flour	pinch salt
3 large eggs	4 pinches saffron
1 teaspoon olive oil	

(TO STEAM THE MUSSELS)

1½ pounds mussels, well-rinsed and de-bearded	1 bay leaf
	1 clove garlic, minced
½ cup dry white wine	

(TO PREPARE THE FENNEL)

1 fresh fennel root	juice of ½ lemon

(TO ASSEMBLE)

1 shallot, minced	2 ounces butter

(TO COOK THE FETTUCCINE)

1 tablespoon salt	¼ teaspoon salt
2 tablespoons olive oil	¼ teaspoon white pepper
the raw fettuccine	the cooked pasta
¼ cup dry white wine	

(PASTA DOUGH)
◆ Sift the flour into a large mixing bowl. Make a well in the center. Add the eggs, olive oil, salt, and saffron. Blend together until the dough comes away from the side of the bowl.
◆ Place the dough on a well-floured surface, and knead at least 10 minutes, until the dough is shiny, smooth, and elastic. Wrap it in plastic and refrigerate it for 30 minutes.
◆ On a floured board, roll the dough out very thin, approximately ¹⁄₃₂-inch thick. Cut it into strips ⅛-inch wide. Place the strips on a pan, keeping them separated so they do not stick together. Set the pan aside.

(TO STEAM THE MUSSELS)
◆ Place the mussels in a pan with the wine, bay leaf, and garlic. Cover the pan. Bring the liquid to a boil, and steam the mussels approximately 5 minutes, or until all have opened. Remove the mussels from their shells. Discard the shells and the liquid.

Making pasta is time-consuming. You may prefer to purchase commercially prepared fettuccine, either dried or fresh (substitute 1 pound fresh or ¼ pound dried). Since saffron pasta may be difficult to find, you might prepare this dish with an unflavored fettuccine, adding the saffron during the fennel and mussel sauté.

Before you cook any pasta, the water should be boiling rapidly; otherwise the final product will be mushy. Stir the pasta around to prevent clumping. After returning the water to a full boil, cook fresh pasta about 1 minute, dried pasta 8 to 10 minutes. If you aren't going to serve the pasta immediately, rinse it in cold water, drain it, and toss it with oil to keep the pieces from sticking together. To reheat the pasta, drop it into boiling water for 30 seconds, then drain it.

(TO PREPARE THE FENNEL)
- Trim the fennel root and cut it into ⅛-by-⅛-by-1-inch julienne strips. Immerse these strips in a bath of the lemon juice and enough cold water to cover the strips.

(TO COOK THE PASTA)
- Add the salt and the olive oil to 1½ gallons water, and bring the water to a boil. Drop the pasta into the water, and bring it back to a boil. Cook the pasta 1 minute, or until it is al dente. Drain the pasta, stir in 1 ounce butter, and set the pasta aside.

(TO ASSEMBLE)
- Sauté the shallot in a large pan with 1 ounce of the butter. Drain the fennel strips, and sauté them with the shallot for 3 minutes. Add the white wine, remaining lemon juice, mussels, salt, and pepper. Simmer until the liquid is reduced by half. Add the pasta and the remaining 1 ounce butter. Toss until the butter is fully incorporated, and serve.

Wine recommendation: 1986 Clos du Bois Chardonnay (California)

Shrimp Sautéed with Tomato and Fresh Herbs

2 ounces butter	½ teaspoon minced fresh
1 shallot, minced	tarragon
20 U/12 shrimp (see page 9),	1 teaspoon minced parsley
peeled and deveined	1 teaspoon minced chives
½ cup dry white wine	1 teaspoon minced fresh
¾ cup peeled, seeded, and	coriander
medium-diced tomatoes	salt and white pepper
(tomato fondue, page 19)	1 ounce butter

- Sauté the shallot in the butter, covered, for 3 minutes. Add the shrimp, and sauté for 1 minute. Add the white wine, and bring the liquid to a boil. Remove the shrimp with a slotted spoon, and set it aside. Continue to simmer until the liquid is reduced by half.
- Return the shrimp to the pan, along with the tomato fondue, herbs, and salt and pepper to taste. Add the butter in small pieces, and *montée* them into the sauce. Adjust the seasoning and serve, accompanied by Rice Pilaf (page 69).

Wine recommendation: 1986 Clos du Bois Chardonnay (California)

To peel tomatoes, bring a pot of water, with some salt added, to a rolling boil. Score an X just though the skin on the bottom of each tomato. Place the tomatoes in the boiling salted water. Leave them 15 seconds, then remove them with a slotted spoon and transfer them to an ice water bath. When they are cool, remove the tomatoes from the ice water and slide off their skins.

To prepare tomato fondue, cut out and discard the cores. Cut each tomato into 8 wedges. With the tip of a paring knife, remove as many of the tomato seeds as possible, and discard them. Cut the tomatoes into a medium dice.

Roasted Lobster in Whiskey, Chive Sauce

1 cup vegetable oil	¼ cup dry white wine
4 lobsters, 1¼ pounds each	1 shallot, minced
1 medium onion, roughly cut	1 bay leaf
1 carrot, roughly cut	½ cup dry white wine
1 rib celery, roughly cut	3 tablespoons minced chives
1 leek, roughly cut	1 cup heavy cream
2 cloves garlic, roughly cut	2 ounces butter
1 sprig thyme, chopped	salt and white pepper
½ cup bourbon sour mash	

- Preheat an oven to 375°F.
- Stun each lobster by piercing the top of the shell with the point of a cook's knife, 1 inch below the eyes.
- Pour the oil into a roasting pan large enough to accommodate the four lobsters, and place the pan in the oven. Leave it in for 10 minutes.
- Carefully place the four lobsters in the pan, upside down, and place the vegetables and thyme on top. Roast for 15 minutes, or until the shells turn bright red.
- Pull the pan out of the oven, and place it on top of the stove. Turn on the fire, and pour the bourbon over the lobsters and vegetables. Ignite very carefully with a lit match. Let flame a minute, then extinguish the flames with the white wine.
- Remove the lobsters, and set them aside. Discard the remaining ingredients in the pan.
- Combine the shallot, the bay leaf, the white wine, and half the minced chives. Simmer until the liquid is reduced by half. Add the cream; simmer until the liquid is reduced by half again. Strain the sauce, then return it to the fire. *Montée* the butter. Season to taste with salt and pepper, and add the remaining chives.
- Place each lobster face down on a cutting board, its tail naturally tucked underneath. While firmly grasping the body with one hand, split the tail in half with a large cook's knife. Tear the two split portions from the body. Pull off the claws, and crack them by hitting them with the heel of the knife, or by using a lobster cracker, which is essentially the same as a nut cracker. Remove the meat from the claws and the tail with a small cocktail fork or nut pick. (Save the body for stock or sauce.)
- Arrange the lobster meat on an appropriate serving plate. Top it with the chive sauce, and serve it hot.

Lobster Strudel, Tomato Armagnac Sauce

(BREAD CRUMBS)
1 ounce butter
1 clove garlic, minced

½ cup dry bread crumbs

(STRUDEL DOUGH)
3 cups flour
¼ teaspoon salt
1 large egg
¾ cup lukewarm water

2 tablespoons vegetable oil
¼ teaspoon cider or white
   vinegar

(FILLING)
2 ounces melted butter
the seasoned bread crumbs
1 pound lobster meat, diced
   medium
½ pound fresh spinach (or
   swiss chard), blanched 10
   seconds, then squeezed dry

⅓ pound *chevre* (goat cheese)
2 teaspoons minced basil
   leaves
pinch each of salt and pepper
1 large egg, beaten with ¼ cup
   water

(TOMATO ARMAGNAC SAUCE)
3 tablespoons olive oil
1 shallot, minced
¼ cup Armagnac
1 cup peeled, seeded, and
   medium-diced tomatoes
   (tomato fondue, page 19)
1 teaspoon fresh thyme leaves

1 teaspoon chopped fresh basil
   leaves
¼ cup white stock of fish
   (page 24)
salt and pepper
1 tablespoon Armagnac

(BREAD CRUMBS)
♦ Melt 1 ounce of the butter, and sauté the garlic and bread crumbs.
  Season this mixture with salt and pepper, and set it aside.

(STRUDEL DOUGH)
♦ Sift the flour and salt into a large bowl. Make a well in the
  center, and add the egg, water, oil, and vinegar. Blend together
  to create a soft dough. Remove the dough to a floured work
  surface, and knead it vigorously for 10 minutes. Put it into a
  clean bowl, slightly oiled, and cover the bowl. Set the bowl aside
  to rest for 30 minutes.
♦ Spread a 3-by-3-foot cloth (tablecloth, apron, or sheet) on a
  worktable. Sprinkle the cloth with flour, and rub the flour into
  the fabric. Roll out the dough on this cloth, into a square about
  12 inches across.
♦ Place an assistant on one side of this dough square; you stand
  on the other side. Both of you slip your hands underneath the
  dough, knuckles up. With a backward rolling motion, gently
  stretch the dough, little by little, until it is paper-thin and roughly
  the size of the cloth underneath. Trim any thick edges.

(FILLING)
♦ Preheat an oven to 375°F.
♦ Brush the entire surface of the dough with the melted butter.
  Sprinkle the bread crumbs over. Evenly spread the lobster, spin-

*Strudel dough can be
somewhat temperamental
when you try to stretch it
paper-thin with the backs of
your hands. Though we make
our own at the Pillar House,
you may wish to substitute a
commercial version. Phyllo, or
filo, is the same kind of
dough; it can be found in the
freezer sections of most
supermarkets.*

*To remove the tiny leaves of a
thyme sprig from the stem,
grasp the top of the stem in
one hand, and slide the
forefinger and thumb of the
other hand down the stem.*

ach, cheese, and seasonings in a 4-inch-wide strip along one side of the dough. Roll the dough around the filling and into a long cylinder. Pinch the ends closed, then brush the top of the cylinder with the beaten egg. Place the cylinder on a lightly greased baking sheet, and bake at 375°F until the pastry is golden brown (about 30 minutes).

(TOMATO ARMAGNAC SAUCE)

♦ Sauté the shallot in the olive oil, covered, for 5 minutes. Add the tomato fondue and herbs. Add the fish stock, and simmer until the liquid is reduced by half. Taking care not to scald yourself, purée the sauce in a food processor on low speed. Return the sauce to the fire, season it to taste with salt and pepper, and bring it to a simmer. Add the Armagnac, and carefully ignite the brandy with a match. Remove the sauce to a holding container, cover it, and set it aside.

♦ Cut the strudel into four portions. Pour the Tomato Armagnac Sauce onto four serving plates. Place portions of the strudel on top of the sauce, and serve.

Wine recommendation: Louis Jadot Mâcon Chardonnay (France)

2 · Soups

STOCKS

White Stock (Chicken)

6 pounds chicken bones, necks and backs
1 whole chicken
1 onion, peeled and cut into eighths
2 stalks celery, roughly cut
1 large carrot, with top removed, scrubbed and roughly cut
4 to 6 leek leaves, well rinsed and roughly cut
2 bay leaves
1 teaspoon peppercorns, white or black, cracked
1 teaspoon fresh thyme leaves
1 bunch parsley stems
optional: ½ teaspoon salt

♦ Rinse the bones and chicken well in cold water.
♦ Rinse all the vegetables. To remove all the sand and soil from the leeks, they should be rinsed and drained at least three times.
♦ Cover the bones and chicken with cold water, 3 to 4 inches above the highest bone. Bring to a simmer, and skim off the fat and impurities.
♦ Add the vegetables, herbs, and spices.
♦ Simmer 1 hour. With a large kitchen fork or pair of tongs, lift out the chicken. Set it aside to cool.
♦ When the chicken has cooled enough to handle, cut it up, and remove all the cooked meat. Wrap and store this meat for use in another dish (such as Pillar House Chicken Salad, pages 35–36). Put the remaining carcass, skin and bones, back into the simmering stock. Continue simmering 4 to 8 hours. Skim off and discard the impurities.
♦ Strain, cool, cover, and refrigerate the stock.

As indicated by its French name, fond *(literally "bottom"), stock is a foundation of good cooking.*

Stocks are made of three elements: nutritional, aromatic, and liquid. The nutritional element consists of bones and meat. The aromatic element is the mirepoix, *plus herbs and spices. A mirepoix is made up of celery, carrots, onions, and sometimes the green tops of leeks; the standard herbs and spices added are peppercorns, bay leaves, thyme leaves, and parsley stems. The liquid element, finally, is generally water, but sometimes wine and roasting pan juices.*

The type of bones used, and whether or not they are roasted, or browned, will determine the dominating flavor of the stock. White stocks, in which the bones and aromatics are added to the liquid without any previous cooking, are lighter in color and flavor than brown stocks. The bones of any of the following may be used in either white or brown stock: beef, veal, chicken, turkey, duck, lamb, and game. Fish bones—from lean, white-fleshed varieties such as sole, halibut, and cod—are used for white stock only. Since fish bones are delicate, only one and a half hours are required to extract their flavor. Also, we may at times combine different types of bones in one stock. This is practical when one has odds and ends from various meals on hand.

Wash the bones and meat well in cold water, then place them in a pot with enough water to cover the highest bone by three or four inches. For maximum extraction of flavor, be sure the water is cold; adding hot water at this point would prematurely seal the pores.

When cooking stocks, a gentle hand is the rule. Stocks should never be boiled, but always simmered. As a stock simmers, fat and impurities will gather on the surface. Periodically skim off these impurities with a ladle. Four to six hours is the minimum amount of time for simmering a stock (with the exception of fish and lobster stock). We recommend the better part of a day, provided one is there throughout the simmering process to keep an eye on it.

Brown Stock (Veal or Beef)

6 to 8 pounds marrow bones of veal, beef, or both, in 3- to 4-inch lengths
2 medium onions, peeled and cut into eighths
2 carrots, scrubbed, with tops removed
2 stalks celery, roughly cut
4 to 6 leek leaves, well rinsed

1 clove garlic, crushed
2 well-ripened tomatoes
2 bay leaves
2 teaspoons black peppercorns, crushed
2 sprigs thyme
1 bunch parsley stems
optional: ½ teaspoon salt

♦ Roast the bones, in a preheated 400°F oven, in a roasting pan for 30 minutes.
♦ Remove the bones to a stockpot, and cover them with cold water, 4 inches over the highest bone. Bring the water to a simmer, and skim.
♦ Place the onions, carrots, celery, leek tops, garlic, and tomatoes in the roasting pan. Return the pan to the oven, and roast the vegetables about 30 minutes, stirring frequently.
♦ After the stock has come to a boil, add the roasted vegetables and the herbs and spices.
♦ Continue simmering 4 to 6 hours, skimming periodically.
♦ Strain, cool, cover, and refrigerate the stock.

Fish Stock

10 pounds white fish bones
1 onion, peeled and cut into eighths
4 leek leaves, well rinsed, roughly cut
3 or 4 mushrooms, roughly cut
1 stalk celery, roughly cut
2 ounces butter

1 bay leaf
½ teaspoon white peppercorns, crushed
2 sprigs thyme
1 bunch parsley stems
2 cups dry white wine
juice of 1 lemon
optional: ¼ teaspoon salt

♦ Soak the bones in cold water for 1 hour. Drain and rinse them, making sure to remove all remnants of entrails and gills.
♦ Place the celery, onions, and leeks in a stockpot with the butter, and sauté for 10 minutes. Add the bones, and sauté 5 minutes more.
♦ Add the wine, the lemon juice, and enough cold water to come 4 inches above the highest bone. Bring to a simmer; skim. Add the herbs and spices, and continue simmering 1½ hours.
♦ Strain, cool, cover, and refrigerate the stock.

Lobster Stock

½ cup olive oil
4 pounds lobster bodies
2 shallots, roughly cut
2 carrots with tops removed,
　scrubbed and roughly cut
2 stalks celery, roughly cut
1 large leek, well rinsed and
　roughly cut

1 bay leaf
4 sprigs thyme
1 cup white wine
optional: 1 teaspoon salt
2 white peppercorns, crushed

- Heat the oil to the smoking point in a large stockpot. Add the lobster bodies. Sauté until the bodies turn bright red. Add the shallots and stir. Add the remaining ingredients and stir well.
- Add enough cold water to cover all the lobster bodies by three inches. Simmer 45 minutes, skimming occasionally.
- Strain, cool, cover, and refrigerate the stock.

COLD SOUPS

Vichyssoise

4 leeks, white part only, well-
　rinsed and chopped
¼ cup roughly cut chives
1 stalk celery, roughly cut
1 shallot, minced
1 clove garlic, minced
2 ounces butter
4 cups peeled and roughly cut
　all-purpose potatoes

1 quart white stock of chicken
　(page 23)
leaves from 2 sprigs thyme,
　chopped
1 bay leaf
1 cup light cream or half and
　half
salt and white pepper
¼ cup minced chives

- In a 1-gallon, heavy-bottomed sauce pan, sauté the leeks, chives, celery, shallot, and garlic in the butter, covered, for 10 minutes. Stir frequently.
- Add the potatoes, and toss the ingredients together over a high flame for 3 minutes.
- Add the chicken stock, thyme, and bay leaf, and simmer for 30 minutes.
- Strain the soup, reserving the liquid and the solids. Remove and discard the bay leaf. Purée the solids in a food processor or food mill. Return the liquid and puréed solids to the sauce pan. While stirring, slowly add the cream. Bring the soup back to a simmer, and season it to taste with salt and white pepper.
- Allow the soup to cool to room temperature, then chill it over-night in the refrigerator.

Once a stock has been strained, it can be returned to the fire and simmered further to reduce, or concentrate it. The longer the reduction, the stronger the flavor of the stock. Taste it now and then to determine when the stock is sufficiently reduced.

When a stock has been finished, allow it to cool before placing it under refrigeration. Putting a hot stock directly into the refrigerator would lower the temperature inside the refrigerator and cause unnecessary condensation. Also, whereas the outermost liquid would chill quickly, this cool layer could insulate a central hot spot—a perfect breeding ground for bacteria that could sour the stock. To hasten cooling, place the container holding the stock in a sink full of ice and water, and periodically stir the stock with a spoon until it is cool to the touch.

Before using a refrigerated stock, turn the fire on high to heat it as quickly as possible. Turn the fire down as soon as the stock begins to simmer.

A chilled stock will often have a gelatinous consistency. The gelatin is derived from the marrow of the bones used. The more gelatinous the stock, the better the flavor.

Crack peppercorns by placing them on a cutting board and pressing and rolling them with the clean bottom of a sauté pan. As one sniff will tell you, this expedites the extraction of their flavor.

Vichyssoise *comes from Vichy, the name of a French town known for its natural spring water and an abundance of health spas. Most of the dishes originating in Vichy (such as Vichy-style carrots, which are sliced thin, simmered in a little Vichy water, and seasoned only with chopped parsley) are regarded as health-restoring.*

As vichyssoise sits overnight, the starch in the potatoes continues to expand. The soup may therefore need to be thinned slightly upon service. Stir in additional cream or, if you are fat-conscious, a bit of chicken stock.

Vichyssoise can also be served hot. In this case it is known as potato soup Jackson.

Ginger beer is not an alcoholic beverage, but rather a more potent variety of ginger ale. Several brands are imported from the West Indies. One, Cock and Bull, is very similar to our ginger ale but has a much stronger presence of ginger and no caramel coloring.

♦ When you are ready to serve the soup, thin it, if necessary, with additional cream or stock. Adjust the seasonings. Serve the vichyssoise in chilled soup bowls or soup plates garnished with the minced chives and a dollop of sour cream, crème fraiche, or plain yoghurt.

Chilled Strawberry Soup

1 quart fresh, ripe strawberries, gently rinsed, tops removed
1 tablespoon grated fresh ginger
2 cups ginger ale or ginger beer
1/4 cup strawberry liqueur
1 tablespoon chopped fresh mint leaves

1/4 teaspoon fresh-grated nutmeg
1/4 teaspoon ground cinnamon
1/8 teaspoon ground cloves
pinch salt
4 tablespoons sour cream
4 mint leaves

♦ Purée all but the sour cream and four mint leaves in a food processor. Chill overnight. Serve in chilled soup bowls, each decorated with a dollop of sour cream and a fresh mint leaf.

Wine recommendation: Mumm's Extra Dry Champagne (France)

HOT SOUPS

French Onion Soup, Gruyère

1 ounce butter
12 medium Spanish onions, sliced
1 clove garlic, minced
1 bay leaf
2 ounces dry sherry
1 pint white stock of chicken (page 23)

1 pint brown stock of beef (page 24)
1/2 teaspoon salt
1/4 teaspoon white pepper
1 2-to-3-inch round slice of stale French bread, lightly toasted
1 cup grated Gruyère cheese

♦ Sauté the onions in the butter, stirring frequently, until they are well caramelized to a dark brown color. Don't let the onions burn.
♦ Stir in the garlic. Add the bay leaf and dry sherry.
♦ Add the chicken and beef stock. Bring the soup to a boil, then down to a simmer. Skim impurities from the top. Continue simmering 20 minutes.

- Season the soup to taste with salt and white pepper. Remove the bay leaf.
- Fill an oven-proof crock or bowl with the soup. Place the toast on top, and sprinkle the grated cheese over. To keep the toast from burning, cover its entire surface with the cheese.
- Place the crock under a broiler, and broil until the cheese is melted and golden brown. Serve immediately.

Wine recommendation: 1986 Montrose Chardonnay (Australia)

Pillar House Clam Chowder

¼ cup salt pork, ground in a meat grinder
¼ cup bacon, ground in a meat grinder
1 medium onion, diced medium
1 stalk celery, diced medium
½ teaspoon minced garlic
1 bay leaf
1 teaspoon fresh thyme leaves
⅛ teaspoon pepper

2 teaspoons flour
3 cups clam juice
1 cup medium-diced potatoes
2 cups small-diced fresh clams (see page 8)
2 cups light cream or half and half
½ teaspoon Worcestershire sauce
salt and pepper

- Render the salt pork and bacon in a covered sauce pan. Avoid browning.
- Add the onion, celery, garlic, bay leaf, thyme, and pepper. Sauté all, covered, for 5 minutes.
- Stir in the flour, and cook for 3 minutes, stirring constantly.
- Add the clam juice, and stir to blend the ingredients. Add the diced potatoes. Add the clams, cream, and Worcestershire. Stir, then simmer until the potatoes are tender. Season the soup to taste with salt and pepper.

Rhode Island Reds' Clam Chowder

1 onion, diced medium
½ cup medium-diced carrot
1 stalk celery, diced medium
1 teaspoon minced garlic
½ cup medium-diced fennel root
1 teaspoon fresh thyme leaves
6 dill stems, tied together
4 ounces butter
1 cup peeled, seeded, and medium-diced tomatoes (tomato fondue, page 19)

¾ cup medium-diced all-purpose potatoes
1 tablespoon Worcestershire sauce
2 cups small-diced fresh clams
4 cups clam juice
2 teaspoons chopped fresh dill leaves
salt and white pepper
4 4-inch round french, kaiser, or poppy seed rolls

This recipe was created in 1975 in honor of The Rhode Island Reds, a professional hockey team.

- In a 1-gallon sauce pan, sauté the onion, carrot, celery, garlic, fennel, thyme, and dill stems in the butter, covered, over a medium flame, for 10 minutes.
- Preheat an oven to 400°F.
- Add the potatoes, Worcestershire, tomatoes, clams, clam juice, and chopped dill. Simmer until the potatoes are tender. Season to taste with the salt and pepper.
- Remove a ½-inch slice from the top of each roll. Tear out the bread from the inside of each roll.
- Place the hollowed rolls and their tops, cut side up on a baking sheet. Bake about 10 minutes, or until they are golden brown.
- Place each hollow roll in a large soup bowl. Ladle the piping-hot soup into the hollow, and cover with the top of the roll.

Clarified butter is used in place of whole butter when only the fat is called for. Whole, or uncooked, butter contains other elements that may brown during cooking. Because clarified butter won't brown, it is preferred in cooking omelettes. It is also served as a dipping sauce for shellfish such as lobster.

To clarify butter, bring it to a boil, then allow it to sit for 15 minutes or so. Ladle off the fat from the top, and discard the milk solids left behind.

Lobster Stew with Mussels

1 pound mussels, de-bearded	1½ quarts lobster stock (page 25)
2 strips bacon	¼ teaspoon salt
1 ounce clarified butter	pinch white pepper
½ large or 1 small onion, diced medium	1¼ cups potatoes, diced medium
1 medium carrot, diced medium	½ cup cooked, medium-diced lobster meat
1 stalk celery, diced medium	¼ cup dry sherry
leaves of 2 sprigs thyme	salt and white pepper to taste
2 basil leaves, chopped	

- Place the mussels in a pot with an inch of water; cover. Bring the water to a boil. Boil 8 to 10 minutes, or until the mussels open. Remove the flesh from the shells. Discard the shells and the water.
- Render the bacon. Remove the solid pieces, and discard them.
- Add the butter, vegetables, and herbs to the bacon fat. Sauté all, covered, for 10 minutes.
- Add the stock, salt, and white pepper, and simmer until the stock is reduced by a third, yielding approximately 1 quart.
- Add the diced potatoes to the stock, and simmer 10 minutes.
- Add the lobster meat, mussels, and sherry.
- Season to taste with salt and white pepper.

Lobster Bisque

2 tablespoons peanut oil
1 1-pound live lobster, cut into
  12 pieces
¾ cup onion, diced medium
¾ cup carrot, diced medium
¾ cup celery, diced medium
1 leek, white part only, well
  rinsed and diced medium
2 sprigs parsley
1 bay leaf

2 teaspoons paprika
2 grinds pepper
½ teaspoon salt
2 tablespoons brandy
1 tablespoon white wine
1 quart heavy cream
salt and pepper
4 ounces bay scallops,
  quartered
¼ cup amontillado sherry

◆ In a 1-gallon sauce pan, heat the peanut oil. Add the lobster pieces, and sauté until all the shells are bright red (about 6 minutes). With a slotted spoon, remove all the lobster pieces, and set them aside.

◆ Add the vegetables, herbs, and spices to the oil. Stir, then cover and cook for 10 minutes. Meanwhile, remove the lobster meat from the tail, claws, and arms. Set the meat aside. Discard the claw shells, but cut up all the other shells, including the body, into pieces no larger than 1-inch square. When the aromatics have finished cooking, add these shell pieces to the pan.

◆ Add the brandy, stand back from the stove, and carefully ignite with a match. After a minute, extinguish with the wine.

◆ Add the cream, simmer, and reduce by half. Run the entire mixture, about 1 cup at a time, through a food processor. Then run the processed mixture through a fine strainer, pressing to extract as much of the liquid as possible. Return the strained soup to the stove, bring it to a simmer, and adjust the seasonings with salt and pepper.

◆ Cut the lobster meat into ¼-inch pieces. Add the lobster and the scallops to the simmering bisque. Finish with the amontillado. Bring the bisque to a simmer, and serve.

Consommé with Ruby Port

3 large egg whites
2 teaspoons kosher salt
1 pound very lean ground veal
  or beef
1 stalk celery, well rinsed, in
  large julienne
1 small leek, well rinsed, in
  large julienne
1 carrot, peeled, in large
  julienne
1 clove garlic, roughly cut

½ teaspoon peppercorns,
  crushed
2 sprigs thyme
1 sprig rosemary
1 bay leaf
1 ripe tomato, diced medium
3 quarts cold, rich beef stock
¼ cup ruby port wine
½ cup blanched small-diced
  vegetables (celery, carrots,
  onions, leeks, zucchini, etc.)

The twelve pieces of lobster called for here are—the claws, each halved; the two arms; the body, quartered; the tail, halved.

To cut up a live lobster, place the heel of a heavy-duty cook's knife against the piece to be cut, then, with the heel of the other hand punch the back of the knife. (If you are unfamiliar with the handling of a cook's knife, use a pair of poultry shears.) Do the cutting over a pan to catch the juices that run out. You can add these juices to the sautéing aromatics.

If the thought of cutting up a live lobster makes you queasy, you may wish to first stun it by piercing the back of its head with a swift insertion of a cook's knife, at a point roughly 1 inch from the front end of its shell.

Lobster shells are hard to break up in a food processor; hence our instruction to first cut all pieces 1-inch square or smaller. Also, be sure the top to the processor is securely in place, and the funnel opening well covered. It is wise to cover the entire apparatus with a damp cloth before turning it on.

Consommé, which becomes a classic soup when garnished and finished with port wine, is an ultra-clarified broth.

The importance of stirring constantly during the initial simmering cannot be overstressed. When the mixture of cold ingredients is placed on the fire, the egg whites tend to remain at the bottom of the pot. Stirring keeps them moving, thus preventing them from burning.

Once the ingredients begin their first slow simmer, the egg whites slowly begin to coagulate. As the heat conduction increases throughout, the stock begins to circulate through the slowly congealing egg whites. As the albumen in the egg whites, supplemented with that in the vegetables and ground meat, becomes firmer and firmer, it traps the impurities in the stock, thus yielding a clear broth. The "raft" is the slowly solidifying mass of egg whites, ground meat, and aromatics that forms at the top of the consommé.

As important as it is to stir initially, it is just as important to stop stirring once the raft begins to form. Otherwise the clarification process would be interrupted.

- Whip the egg whites and the salt until the whites are frothy.
- In a 2-gallon, heavy-gauge stockpot, blend the egg whites with all the other ingredients except the stock.
- Add the cold beef stock, and stir well.
- Over maximum heat, stir the mixture constantly until it just begins to simmer.
- Discontinue stirring, and simmer *very slowly* for 1 hour.
- With a perforated spoon, very gently lift out a section of the "raft," and discard it. The clear broth will be exposed through this opening.
- Gently ladle out the broth, endeavoring not to disturb the remaining raft. Stain the broth through a very fine strainer or through a piece of cheesecloth or muslin lining a coarser strainer.
- When all the broth has been ladled from the stockpot, discard the raft.
- Lay a paper towel on top of the broth. Lift the paper, and discard it. Repeat this until all the fat is gone from the top of the hot broth.
- Bring the broth back to a boil. Stir in the ruby port wine, ladle the broth into soup bowls, and garnish with the small-diced vegetables.

Lobster and Scallop Mousse, Sweet Red Pepper Purée

French Onion Soup, Gruyère, and Seafood Omelette

Grapefruit and Avocado Salad, Raspberry-Honey Vinaigrette

Pillar House Chicken Salad

Grilled Swordfish, Tomato-Coriander Butter

Poached Filet of Salmon, Lemon-Thyme Sauce, with Steamed Broccoli

Breast of Chicken Côte d'Azur

Grilled Breast of Duckling, Mango-Port Sauce

Medallions of Veal, Ragout of Wild Mushrooms, and Marsala Cream

Roulade of Veal, Garlic-Herb-Ricotta Stuffing

Roast Rack of Lamb, Rosemary-Pommery Sauce

Chateaubriand, Bouquet of Seasonal Vegetables

Left to right: Pecan Rolls, Dill and Onion Rolls, Gingered Biscuits, and Anadama Bread

Reine de Saba and Strawberry Millefeuille with Strawberry Sauce

Mixed Fruit Tart and Chocolate Pâté, Pistachio Sauce

Pecan Tart and Apple Pie with Vermont Cheese

3 · Salads

APPETIZER SALADS

Marinated Mushrooms, Belgian Endive, and Bibb Lettuce

Feel free to substitute other wild mushrooms for the shitakes, chanterelles, and enokis called for here (see page 12).

(MUSHROOMS)
1 cup fresh button mushrooms
1 cup fresh shitake mushrooms
1 cup fresh chanterelle mushrooms
1 package (about ½ cup) fresh enoki mushrooms
juice of 1 lemon

(MARINADE)
¾ cup olive oil
¼ cup red wine vinegar
¼ cup dry white wine
¼ teaspoon salt
¼ teaspoon white pepper
2 tablespoons minced garlic
1 shallot, minced
1 sprig rosemary
2 sprigs thyme
1 sprig oregano
4 dashes Tabasco sauce
2 teaspoons dijon mustard
1 bay leaf

(TO ASSEMBLE)
8 large bibb lettuce leaves
4 cupped leaves of red cabbage
the marinated mushrooms
16 belgian endive leaves
¼ cup minced parsley

(MUSHROOMS)
♦ Trim the ends of the stems on all the mushrooms. Add the lemon juice to a bowl of cold water, and rinse the mushrooms gently in this bath. Remove them, and pat them dry.

(MARINADE)
♦ Bring to a boil all the marinade ingredients. Remove the marinade from the fire.

◆ Place the mushrooms in a container with the marinade. Allow the mixture to cool, then refrigerate it for 24 hours.

(TO ASSEMBLE)
◆ Arrange the bibb lettuce on chilled plates. Place the red cabbage cups in the center, and fill them each with a portion of the marinated mushrooms. Arrange 4 belgian endive leaves around each cabbage cup. Top the mushrooms with minced parsley.

Spinach and Feta Cheese, Warm Bacon Dressing

(CROUTONS)
1 clove garlic, minced
1½ ounces butter
4 slices white bread, their crusts removed, cut into ¼-inch cubes

pinch each of salt, white pepper, and paprika

(DRESSING)
½ pound bacon, diced small
1 onion, minced
1 clove garlic, minced

¼ cup cider vinegar
4 tablespoons honey
¼ cup orange juice

(TO ASSEMBLE)
1 pound spinach leaves, well washed, dried, and torn into bite-size pieces
¼ cup grated carrot

the dressing
¼ cup crumbled feta cheese
the croutons

(CROUTONS)
◆ Sauté the garlic in the butter for 1 minute. Add the bread cubes, salt, white pepper, and paprika. Stir well, and continue sautéing and stirring until the bread cubes are golden brown. Remove them to absorbent paper.

(DRESSING)
◆ Cook the bacon in a sauté pan until it is lightly browned. Remove it with a slotted spoon to absorbent paper.
◆ Sauté the onion and garlic in the remaining bacon fat for 4 minutes. Drain off the fat, and discard it.
◆ Combine the remaining dressing ingredients in a small sauce pan, and simmer for 5 minutes. Add the bacon, onion, and garlic, and remove the pan from the fire. Set it aside.

(TO ASSEMBLE)
◆ Place the spinach leaves and grated carrot in a large bowl. Add the warm dressing, and toss. Arrange the spinach on serving plates, and top with the crumbled feta and the croutons.

Caesar Salad

(DRESSING)

3 cloves garlic, minced
½ teaspoon dijon mustard
4 anchovy filets, minced
3 tablespoons lemon juice
4 dashes Tabasco sauce

2 dashes Worcestershire sauce
pinch each of salt and white
　pepper
1 large egg
1½ cups olive oil

(TO ASSEMBLE)

1 large head romaine lettuce,
　rinsed, dried, and cut across
　the width of each leaf into
　1-inch strips

1 cup croutons (page 32)
the dressing
½ cup grated parmesan cheese
4 anchovy filets, diced small

(DRESSING)

♦ Put the garlic, mustard, anchovies, Tabasco, Worcestershire, salt, pepper, and egg in a blender. Turn the blender on on medium speed, and pour in the olive oil in a slow, steady stream. As the sauce begins to emulsify, alternate the lemon juice with the olive oil.

(TO ASSEMBLE)

♦ Place the romaine pieces in a large bowl, along with the croutons and half the grated parmesan. Add three-quarters of the dressing, and toss.
♦ Arrange the salad on serving plates, and sprinkle the remaining cheese and the diced anchovy filets over. Top with additional dressing as needed.

Wine recommendation: 1982 Schramsberg Blanc de Noir (California)

Grapefruit and Avocado Salad, Raspberry-Honey Vinaigrette

(RASPBERRY-HONEY VINAIGRETTE)

1 pint fresh raspberries
¼ cup white vinegar
¼ cup dry white wine

4 tablespoons honey
¼ teaspoon salt

(TO ASSEMBLE)

1 small pink grapefruit, peeled
　and cut into 16 to 20
　skinned and seeded wedges
2 ripe avocados, peeled and
　cut into 8 wedges each

Raspberry-Honey Vinaigrette
12 raspberries
4 small bunches seedless red
　grapes
1 sprig mint

There are probably as many different recipes for Caesar salad as there are captains and maitre d's preparing them in restaurant and hotel dining rooms around the world. And there are numerous tales regarding the origin of this dish. One involves a maitre d' named Caesar in a Mexican inn in the early part of this century. A huge banquet was underway, and some of the food supplies ordered had not arrived on time. Unfazed, Caesar substituted the planned salad with one composed of ingredients on hand—romaine lettuce, stale bread, anchovies, olive oil, eggs, and so on. At table side in the dining room, the stale bread was turned into golden-brown croutons, and the salad was tossed. Because of all the fanfare that accompanied the salad's creation, none of the guests were disappointed at the unannounced substitution.

Gently rinse lettuce in plenty of ice-cold water to remove all sand and soil. Dry it thoroughly; wet lettuce will water down an accompanying sauce or vinaigrette. To dry lettuce, spin it in a lettuce spinner, then wrap it in absorbent paper and place it in a plastic bag in the refrigerator, or wrap it in a clean pillowcase and refrigerate it.

After it is dry, delicate lettuce, such as butter, red leaf, or green leaf, should be separated leaf by leaf, then torn into bite-size pieces by hand. Coarser lettuce, such as iceberg or romaine, yields a better presentation when cut with a knife into uniform pieces.

(RASPBERRY-HONEY VINAIGRETTE)

♦ Purée all the ingredients in a food processor. Cover and refrigerate until the salad is ready to serve.

(TO ASSEMBLE)

♦ Arrange the grapefruit and avocado wedges in a pinwheel pattern on four individual plates. Top them with the vinaigrette, and garnish with three raspberries each and two or three mint leaves.

Mozzarella, Prosciutto, and Tomato, Lemon-Basil Vinaigrette

A dry-cured, chewy ham, prosciutto can be sliced to order at almost any delicatessen counter.

(LEMON-BASIL VINAIGRETTE)

2 shallots, minced	½ teaspoon salt
½ cup minced fresh basil	½ teaspoon white pepper
¾ cup olive oil	2 tablespoons balsamic vinegar
¼ cup lemon juice	

(TO ASSEMBLE)

½ pound mozzarella cheese, cut into 12 to 16 slices	Lemon-Basil Vinaigrette
12 paper-thin slices prosciutto	
2 large vine-ripened beefsteak tomatoes, cut into 8 slices each	

(LEMON-BASIL VINAIGRETTE)

♦ Purée all of the vinaigrette ingredients in a food processor. Allow them to marinate, refrigerated, for 24 hours.

(TO ASSEMBLE)

♦ Arrange alternate slices of mozzarella, prosciutto, and tomato on four individual serving plates, and top with the vinaigrette.

ENTRÉE SALADS

Smoked Turkey with Avocado

We get our smoked turkey breast from North Country Smokehouse in Claremont, New Hampshire.

1 pound smoked turkey breast, in 1-by-⅛-by-⅛-inch julienne	16 thin round slices cucumber
	1 head bibb lettuce
2 ripe avocados, halved, peeled, and pitted	½ cup whole-grain Pommery mustard
1 ripe tomato, cut into 8 wedges	

- Place the avocado halves cut side down on a cutting surface. Slice them lengthwise into ⅛-inch pieces. Do not separate the slices.
- Arrange the bibb lettuce leaves on four serving plates. Place an avocado half in the center of each. Press down and to one side, so the avocado fans out. Sprinkle the julienned turkey on one side of each avocado half, and the cucumber slices and tomato wedges on the other. Serve the whole-grain mustard separately.

Salmon Tortellini, Lemon-Basil Vinaigrette

Salmon Tortellini (pages 13–14)
1 tablespoon salt

2 tablespoons olive oil
Lemon-Basil Vinaigrette (page 34)

If you prefer, substitute commercially made tortellini, fresh or frozen, with a cheese filling. Add flaked poached salmon to the dish along with the Lemon-Basil Vinaigrette.

- In a large pot, add the salt and olive oil to 1½ gallons water. Bring the water to a rapid boil. Add the tortellini, bring the water to a boil again, and cook until the pasta is al dente.
- Drain the tortellini, place it in a large bowl, and toss it with the vinaigrette. Let it cool to room temperature, then refrigerate it until you are ready to serve it.

Pillar House Chicken Salad

2 6-ounce boned, skinned chicken breast halves
1 cup dry white wine
½ cup water
1 bay leaf
pinch each of salt and pepper
1 cup green beans, trimmed at ends, split lengthwise, and cut into ¼-inch lengths
1 cup grated carrot
½ cup grated celeriac (celery root)

½ cup mayonnaise
juice of 2 small lemons
salt and white pepper to taste
1 small head bibb lettuce
1 small head radicchio
1 ripe tomato, cut into 8 wedges
2 hard-cooked eggs, cut into 4 wedges each
16 niçoise or calamata olives

Splitting green beans lengthwise is a technique developed to substitute for the very thin green beans, haricots verts, grown in France.

- In a sauce pan, bring the wine, water, bay leaf, and pinch each of salt and pepper to a boil. Add the chicken breasts, cover, and simmer for 10 minutes. Remove them, and pat them dry. Cut them into ½-inch chunks, and set them aside.
- Blanch the green beans in boiling salted water until they are tender, but al dente—about 6 minutes. Drain them, and set them aside.
- Combine the chicken, green beans, carrots, celeriac, mayonnaise, lemon juice, and salt and white pepper to taste in a large mixing bowl. Stir together until the ingredients are well blended. Refrigerate the mixture until you are ready to serve the salad.

♦ Remove the core from the bibb lettuce, and separate the leaves. Arrange the lettuce leaves on four individual plates. Arrange two or three radicchio leaves over each base of lettuce. Mound about a quarter of the chicken salad in the center. Garnish with the tomato wedges, egg wedges, and olives.

Wine recommendation: Crossroad's Vineyard Scrimshaw White (California)

Chef's Seafood Salad

(RÉMOULADE)

2 large egg yolks
2 tablespoons dijon mustard
pinch each of salt and pepper
4 teaspoons chopped parsley
1 anchovy filet, mashed
1 cup olive oil

juice of ½ lemon
2 tablespoons white wine
  vinegar or cider vinegar
1 tablespoon capers, drained
¼ cup sour gherkins, diced
  small

(TO COOK THE SHRIMP AND SCALLOPS)

12 16/20 count shrimp (see
  page 9)
½ cup dry white wine
½ cup water

1 bay leaf
juice of ½ lemon
pinch each of salt and pepper
1 cup bay scallops

(TO MIX THE SHELLFISH)

the cooked shrimp and scallops
1 cup cooked lobster meat,
  diced medium
1 cup prepared crab meat (any
  variety), shredded

the rémoulade
¼ cup lemon juice
salt and pepper

(TO ASSEMBLE)

1 small head bibb lettuce
1 small head radicchio
the shellfish mixture
1 ripe tomato, cut into 8
  wedges

2 hard-cooked eggs, each cut
  into 4 wedges
1 large lemon, cut into 8
  wedges and seeded
the remaining rémoulade

(RÉMOULADE)

♦ Put the yolks, mustard, salt, pepper, parsley, and anchovy into a food processor, and turn on the machine. Add the olive oil, in a slow, steady stream, alternately with the lemon juice and the vinegar. Continue until all the olive oil, lemon juice, and vinegar has been added, and an emulsified sauce results. Remove the sauce from the processor to a bowl, and blend in the capers and diced gherkins.

(TO COOK THE SHRIMP AND SCALLOPS)

♦ Peel the shrimp. Score the back of each with a sharp paring knife, and rinse the channel under cold running water.

♦ Bring the wine, water, bay leaf, lemon, salt, and pepper to a boil. Place the shrimp and scallops in this liquid, bring it back to a boil, and remove it from the fire. Allow it to sit 8 to 10 minutes.

♦ Drain the shrimp and scallops, and pat them dry.

(TO MIX THE SHELLFISH)

♦ Dice the shrimp into ¼-inch pieces. Cut the scallops into quarters. Place the shrimp, scallops, lobster, and crab in a large mixing bowl. Add enough rémoulade to bind the shellfish together. Add the lemon juice, season to taste with salt and pepper and stir until all ingredients are well mixed.

(TO ASSEMBLE)

♦ Arrange the lettuce leaves on four individual plates. Arrange the radicchio leaves on top of these. Divide the shellfish mixture among the four plates. Garnish with the tomato wedges, egg wedges, and lemon wedges. Serve the remaining rémoulade separately.

Ray West fillets a flounder at Captain Marden's Seafood in Wellesley, Massachusetts.

4 ◆ *Main Courses*

FISH AND SHELLFISH

Baked Haddock, Seafood Stuffing

1 small onion, roughly cut
1 stalk celery, roughly cut
1 small carrot, peeled and roughly cut
1 small leek, white part only, well rinsed and roughly cut
1 shallot, roughly cut
½ pound butter
½ cup halibut or sole filet, poached and flaked
¼ cup flaked crab meat (any variety)
¼ cup titi shrimp (cooked baby shrimp)

½ teaspoon fresh thyme leaves
½ cup minced parsley
1 cup fresh white bread crumbs
¾ cup crushed Ritz crackers
¾ cup clarified butter
¼ cup dry sherry
salt and pepper
4 6-ounce boneless haddock filets
¼ cup dry white wine
¼ cup water

◆ Purée the onion, celery, carrot, leek, and shallot in a food processor. Sauté the mixture in the butter 10 minutes. Transfer it to a large mixing bowl. Add the halibut or sole, crab meat, shrimp, thyme, and parsley.

◆ Add the bread crumbs, cracker crumbs, clarified butter, and sherry. Blend well. Season to taste with salt and pepper.

◆ Preheat an oven to 425°F.

◆ Make a lengthwise incision down the center of each haddock filet, three-quarters of the way through the flesh.

◆ Divide the stuffing into four equal portions. Open the incision on each filet, and insert a portion of the stuffing.

◆ Lightly butter a baking pan, and place the four stuffed filets in it. Pour the white wine and the water into the pan, cover the pan with aluminum foil, and place it in the oven. Bake 10 to 12 minutes.

Broiled Schrod, Lemon-Basil Butter

4 ounces butter, softened
juice of 1 lemon
2 tablespoons fresh basil
   leaves, chopped fine
salt and pepper
4 6-ounce boned and skinned
   schrod filets

¼ cup seasoned dry bread
   crumbs
1 tablespoon melted butter
¼ cup white wine
¼ cup water

- Place the softened butter in a small bowl with the lemon juice, basil, and salt and pepper to taste. Stir with a wooden spoon until the ingredients are well blended. Place the butter on a sheet of wax paper, and roll it into a cylinder. Place it in the refrigerator to chill.
- Preheat an oven to 425°F.
- Top the fish filets with the seasoned bread crumbs, and dribble the melted butter on top. Place the filets in a lightly buttered baking dish with the white wine and water. Bake 8 to 10 minutes, or until the fish is white and flaky throughout.

Wine recommendation: 1986 Commonwealth Vineyards Chardonnay Reserve (Massachusetts)

Grilled Seafood Brochette

1 large egg
¼ teaspoon fresh thyme leaves
¼ teaspoon minced fresh sage
   leaves
¼ teaspoon minced fresh
   coriander leaves
2 small cloves garlic, minced
½ cup olive oil
¼ teaspoon salt
¼ teaspoon white pepper
2 teaspoons rice vinegar

2 tablespoons sake (Japanese
   rice wine)
½ pound swordfish
½ pound fresh tuna
8 large sea scallops
1 red bell pepper
1 small onion
1 ear corn
8 16/20 count shrimp (see page
   9), in their shells
4 large cherry tomatoes

- Place the egg, herbs, garlic, salt, and pepper in a blender. Turn the blender on slow speed, and begin pouring in the olive oil in a slow, steady stream. Alternate the oil with the vinegar and sake. If this marinade becomes too thick, thin it with water, a teaspoon at a time.
- Cut the swordfish and tuna each into eight equal pieces. Cut the bell pepper in half, remove the seeds and ribbing, and cut each half into four equal pieces. Peel the onion, and cut it into eighths. Remove the husk and silk from the ear of corn, and cut it into eight equal pieces.

Commercial fishermen make a long journey to an area off the coast of New England known as Georges Bank, one of the richest fishing grounds in the world. As the fish are caught in the nets, they are stored below, packed in ice. After three to six sixteen-hour days of netting, the boat begins the three-day journey back to the piers, where the fish is auctioned off.

In the late nineteenth century, some of the more opulent of Boston's hotels demanded fish from only the top layers of each catch. Since it was impossible to determine just what variety would end up on top, a generic name evolved for this freshest of the fresh fish. The generic name was schrod.

Today it is generally agreed that schrod is a cod or haddock filet weighing 2½ pounds or less.

To make seasoned dry bread crumbs, break up some stale white bread, and put it into a food processor. Add salt, pepper, a little paprika, and any other herb or spice you choose, such as tarragon, basil, thyme, garlic, or nutmeg. Use your imagination and experiment with different blends.

Make a double or triple quantity of Lemon-Basil Butter if you want to blend it in a food processor. Well wrapped, this and other compound butters keep for several weeks in the refrigerator and up to 3 months in the freezer.

Make sure the scallops you buy are all large and whole. Small pieces will not stay on the skewers.

There is nothing quite as savory as meat, poultry, fish, or vegetables grilled over an open fire. In recent years mesquite charcoal and mesquite chips, usually imported from Mexico, have come into vogue, but many other woods can add an outdoor flavor.

Start an outdoor grill with standard charcoal briquets and an odorless liquid fire starter. Allow a half-hour for the fire to peak, then another half-hour for the fire's heat to diminish slightly. At this point the coals will produce an even heat and will tend not to flame up during grilling.

About twenty minutes before you are ready to start grilling, place some aromatic wood on top of the briquets. You might try alderwood, hickory, or even grapevine cuttings. Packaged wood chips are often available at hardware and garden shops.

Available year-round in many produce markets, coriander is sometimes labeled with its Spanish name, cilantro. *It also goes by the names* Italian parsley *and* Chinese parsley, *due to its common use in the cuisines of Italy and China. It should not be confused with flat-leafed parsley, which looks very much like coriander and is also sometimes referred to as Italian parsley. Flat-leafed parsley is a true form of parsley.*

Don't settle for buying coriander leaves in their dried form, which has virtually none of the aroma or flavor of the fresh.

♦ Drop the corn sections into boiling salted water, and blanch them for 3 minutes. Remove them, and set them aside.

♦ Prepare an outdoor grill or an indoor broiler. If you are using a broiler, set the temperature low, about 300°F.

♦ Push the shrimp, fish, scallops, and vegetables onto metal skewers, alternating the fish and shellfish with the vegetables. Brush liberally with the grilling marinade.

♦ Place the full skewers on the outdoor grill, or on a cookie pan under the broiler. Cook approximately 12 minutes, turning each brochette every 3 to 4 minutes. Serve with Rice Pilaf (page 69).

Wine recommendation: 1986 Maître d'Estournel (France)

Grilled Swordfish, Tomato-Coriander Butter

(TOMATO-CORIANDER BUTTER)

½ pound unsalted butter, softened	2 teaspoons chopped fresh coriander leaves
1 cup peeled, seeded, and medium-diced tomatoes (tomato fondue, page 19)	1 tablespoon dry white wine pinch each of salt and white pepper

(TO PREPARE THE SWORDFISH)

4 6- to 7-ounce swordfish steaks	vegetable oil Tomato-Coriander Butter
salt and white pepper	

(TOMATO-CORIANDER BUTTER)

♦ Put the butter, tomatoes, coriander, wine, salt, and pepper into a food processor, and blend well. Remove the butter mixture to a piece of waxed paper, and roll it into a cylinder roughly 2 inches in diameter. Place the wrapped cylinder in the refrigerator.

(TO PREPARE THE SWORDFISH)

♦ Ready an outdoor grill for grilling. When the coals are ready, season the steaks with salt and pepper, brush them liberally with oil, and place them on the grill. Cook them 3 to 4 minutes on each side.

♦ Remove the steaks to a serving platter. Top each with a slice of the chilled Tomato-Coriander Butter.

Wine recommendation: 1986 Sonoma-Cutrer (California)

Grilled Tuna with Native Crab and Corn

(NATIVE CRAB AND CORN SAUCE)
1 shallot, minced
½ ounce butter
¼ cup dry vermouth
1 cup Fish Stock (page 24)

1 cup heavy cream
½ cup cooked rock crab meat
⅓ cup whole-kernel corn
salt and white pepper

(MARINADE)
1 large egg
¼ teaspoon fresh thyme leaves
¼ teaspoon minced fresh sage
  leaves
¼ teaspoon minced fresh
  coriander leaves
2 cloves garlic, minced

¼ teaspoon salt
¼ teaspoon white pepper
2 teaspoons rice vinegar
½ cup olive oil
2 tablespoons sake (Japanese
  rice wine)

(TO PREPARE THE TUNA)
4 6-ounce center-cut tuna
  steaks

the marinade
Native Crab and Corn Sauce

(NATIVE CRAB AND CORN SAUCE)
◆ Sauté the shallot in the butter, covered, for 3 minutes. Add the
  vermouth, and reduce by half.
◆ Add the fish stock and the cream. Simmer, and reduce by half.
◆ Add the crab meat and the corn. Season to taste with salt and
  pepper.
◆ Remove the sauce from the fire. Transfer it to a holding con-
  tainer, cover it, and set it aside in a warm place.

(MARINADE)
◆ Put the egg, herbs, garlic, salt, pepper, and rice vinegar into a
  blender. Turn the machine on low, and *very slowly* add the olive
  oil, in a steady stream. Add the sake, a teaspoon at a time,
  alternately with the olive oil.

(TO PREPARE THE TUNA)
◆ Liberally brush each tuna steak with the marinade. Cook on an
  outdoor barbecue, or on a baking sheet under a broiler. Allow
  3 to 4 minutes on each side, basting when the steaks are turned
  over.
◆ Serve each steak topped with ¼ cup of the sauce.

Wine recommendation: 1983 Mondavi Reserve Fumé Blanc (California)

If fresh corn is available, shuck an ear, rinse it, and blanch it in boiling salted water for 6 to 8 minutes. Drain and cool the ear, and remove the kernels by holding the ear vertically and cutting downward with a paring knife. In the absence of fresh corn, use frozen whole kernels. They are generally excellent, as they are processed and frozen at their peak of flavor.

This dish was created by Chef Alan Gibson for the 1988 Anthony Spinazzola Scholarship Foundation benefit at Boston University.

The salmon filets are wrapped in the plastic to keep them moist. This is also a precautionary measure used by professionals to compensate for imperfect timing. If the rest of the dinner is not quite ready to serve when the salmon is, simply turn off the fire under the court bouillon, and leave the filets in this poaching medium until you are ready to serve everything. The salmon will remain moist and warm until unwrapped.

Poached Filet of Salmon, Lemon-Thyme Sauce

(COURT BOUILLON)

4 sprigs thyme	1 stalk celery
1 quart dry white wine	1 bunch parsley stems
2 cups water	½ teaspoon salt
1 bay leaf	1 carrot, peeled and roughly
½ teaspoon white peppercorns, crushed	chopped

(LEMON-THYME SAUCE)

3 sprigs thyme	yolks of 4 large eggs
juice of 1 lemon	½ pound clarified butter, very
2 tablespoons dry white wine	warm
2 tablespoons white wine vinegar	salt to taste

(TO PREPARE THE SALMON)

the court bouillon	Lemon-Thyme Sauce
4 6-ounce skinned and boned salmon filets	

(COURT BOUILLON)
- Bring the bouillon ingredients to a boil, and simmer for 5-10 minutes. Remove the pan from the fire, and set it aside.

(LEMON-THYME SAUCE)
- Combine the thyme, lemon juice, white wine, and vinegar in a small pan. Bring the liquid to a simmer, and reduce it by half. Remove the pan from the fire, and set it aside to cool. Strain the mixture.
- Put the egg yolks and the thyme, lemon, and wine mixture into the clean jar of a blender. Turn the blender on low, and slowly pour the heated clarified butter into the whipping eggs. As the sauce begins to thicken, increase the blender speed. If needed, thin the sauce with hot water, a tablespoon at a time. Season to taste with salt. Remove the sauce to a small bowl. Cover the bowl, and set it aside in a warm place.

(TO PREPARE THE SALMON)
- Strain the court bouillon, and bring it to a simmer. Tightly wrap each of the salmon filets in plastic wrap, and gently drop them into the simmering bouillon. Be sure the bouillon covers the filets. Poach them for about 6 minutes. Remove and unwrap the filets.
- Serve them each topped with Lemon-Thyme Sauce and garnished with a sprig of fresh thyme.

Wine recommendation: 1987 Pine Ridge Chenin Blanc (California)

Broiled Chatham Scallops

(CRACKER CRUMB TOPPING)
6 tablespoons Ritz cracker
  crumbs
2 ounces melted butter

¼ cup dry sherry
pinch each of salt and pepper

(TO ASSEMBLE AND COOK)
2 ounces melted butter
1½ pounds Chatham (Cape
  Cod) scallops

2 tablespoons dry sherry
¼ cup dry white wine
Cracker Crumb Topping

♦ Preheat a broiler.

(CRACKER CRUMB TOPPING)
♦ In a small bowl, blend together the cracker crumbs, butter, sherry, salt, and pepper.

(TO ASSEMBLE AND COOK)
♦ Use some of the melted butter to lightly grease 4 small ovenproof casseroles. Divide the scallops among the casseroles. Sprinkle the remaining butter, along with the sherry and the white wine, over the scallops. Broil 3 to 5 minutes.
♦ Sprinkle each casserole with the cracker crumb mixture, return it to the broiler, and lightly brown the top. This will take less than a minute. Serve.

Wine recommendation: 1986 Kenwood Chenin Blanc (California)

Salmon and Chicken Roasted in Olive Oil

½ cup olive oil
1 teaspoon fresh thyme leaves
1 teaspoon fresh rosemary
1 teaspoon minced fresh basil
  leaves
1 tablespoon minced parsley
¼ teaspoon salt

¼ teaspoon fresh-ground
  pepper
½ cup dry white wine
4 6-ounce boned and skinned
  salmon filets
4 6-ounce boned and skinned
  chicken breast halves

♦ In a blender, mix the olive oil, herbs, salt, pepper, and wine. Marinate the salmon filets and chicken breasts 24 hours in this mixture, turning them occasionally.
♦ Preheat an oven to 425°F.
♦ Put a little of the olive oil from the marinade in a cast iron skillet or sauté pan, and place the pan on the fire. Drop the chicken breasts into the hot oil, and sear them on both sides until they are golden brown. Remove them to a roasting pan.
♦ Add the salmon filets to the roasting pan, and roast all at 425°F for 10 to 12 minutes. Remove the filets and breasts, and serve.

To make your own fettuccine, see pages 18–19.

Lobster and Scallops with Champagne Sauce on Fettuccine

(CHAMPAGNE SAUCE)
1 large shallot, minced
1 ounce clarified butter (see page 28)
1 cup dry champagne

1 sprig thyme
¼ vanilla bean, split
1 pint heavy cream
salt and pepper to taste

(TO COOK THE SHELLFISH)
1 teaspoon minced garlic
2 ounces unsalted butter
2 cups sea scallops
1½ cups cooked lobster meat

1 teaspoon chopped fresh basil leaves
1 sprig thyme, chopped
Champagne Sauce

(TO ASSEMBLE)
1 tablespoon salt
2 tablespoons olive oil
1 pound fresh saffron fettuccine

1 ounce butter
the Champagne Sauce and shellfish mixture

(CHAMPAGNE SAUCE)
- Sauté the minced shallot in the butter, covered, for 1 minute.
- Add the champagne, thyme, and vanilla bean. Simmer, and reduce by a third. Add the cream, simmer, and reduce by half. Season with salt and pepper, strain, cover, and set aside.

(TO COOK THE SHELLFISH)
- Sauté the garlic in the butter for 1 minute. *Do not* brown.
- Add the sea scallops, and continue sautéing another 3 minutes. Add the lobster meat and herbs, and continue sautéing about another minute.
- Add the Champagne Sauce, stir, and set aside.

(TO ASSEMBLE)
- Bring 1½ gallons water, with the salt and olive oil, to a rapid boil. Add the fettuccine, stirring immediately to keep the pasta from clumping. Bring the water back to a rapid boil, and continue boiling until the pasta is cooked al dente.
- Strain the pasta, and shake it dry. Remove it to a large bowl, and add the butter and about ¼ cup of the Champagne Sauce and shellfish mixture.
- Serve the pasta on individual plates or on a large platter, topped with the warmed sauce with lobster and scallops.

Wine recommendation: Moët and Chandon Brut (France)

Baked Stuffed Gulf Shrimp

(SEAFOOD STUFFING)
1 medium onion, peeled
1 medium carrot, with top removed, peeled
1 stalk celery
2 cloves garlic
1 shallot, peeled
1 pound unsalted butter
1 bay leaf
1 teaspoon minced fresh thyme

½ teaspoon salt
¼ teaspoon white pepper
½ pound boned and skinned haddock or sole filet
1 cup Ritz cracker crumbs
1 cup fresh white bread crumbs
¼ cup dry sherry

(TO ASSEMBLE)
20 raw U/12 shrimp (see page 9), in their shells
Seafood stuffing
2 ounces melted butter
½ cup water

(SEAFOOD STUFFING)

♦ Purée the onion, carrot, celery, garlic, and shallot in a food processor. In a large sauce pan over a low fire, sauté these vegetables, plus the bay leaf, thyme, salt, and pepper, with the butter, covered, for 30 minutes. Strain, reserving the butter and discarding the vegetables.

♦ Return the butter to the fire. Add the haddock or sole, and sauté until the fish is fully cooked. Add the remaining stuffing ingredients. Stir, allowing the fish to break into small pieces, and blend well. Set the stuffing aside to cool.

(TO ASSEMBLE)

♦ Remove the shell from each shrimp, leaving the last tail section intact. Score the back of each shrimp with a sharp paring knife, rinse out the channel, and discard the entrails. Pat the shrimp dry, and set them aside.

♦ Preheat an oven to 425°F.

♦ Form the stuffing into twenty 2-ounce spheres. Tuck each sphere into the inner curve of a shrimp's body, pressing the shell at the end of the shrimp into the stuffing.

♦ Use some of the melted butter to grease a baking dish or small, individual casseroles. Add the shrimp, and brush them with the remaining melted butter. Pour 2 tablespoons water into each individual casserole, or ½ cup water into the large baking dish. Bake at 425°F for 8 to 10 minutes, and serve.

Wine recommendation: 1986 Dry Creek Fumé Blanc (California)

Baked Maine Lobster, Seafood Stuffing

*Two variations of this recipe
are often welcome for their
simplicity:*

*To broil a lobster, split it
from head to tail on the
underside, sprinkle it with salt
and pepper, top with
seasoned dry bread crumbs
(page 39), and drizzle with
melted butter. Place the
lobster in a roasting pan, with
¼ inch water, in a preheated
400°F oven. Bake 12 to 15
minutes, then brown under
the broiler just before serving.*

*An even simpler dish is
boiled lobster. Drop the
lobster into boiling water,
return the water to a boil,
and simmer 5 minutes.
Remove the pot from the fire,
and let it sit 10 minutes. The
lobster's flesh should be firm
but slightly translucent.
(Overcooking lobster, as all
shellfish, renders it rubbery.)*

6 1¾-pound lobsters
½ cup cooked snow crab meat
½ cup cooked lobster meat
1 cup raw sea scallops

Seafood Stuffing (page 45)
½ cup seasoned dry bread
  crumbs (see page 39)
½ pound butter, melted

♦ Preheat an oven to 350°F.
♦ Split each lobster by cutting the body and the tail down the
  center of the underside (stun the lobster first, if you wish, by
  piercing the back of its head with a cook's knife about 1 inch
  from the front of its shell). Press the lobster open. Remove the
  entrails and the sand sac, a small piece of cartilage-like material.
♦ Distribute the crab meat, cooked lobster meat, and scallops among
  the four lobster bodies. Top with the seafood stuffing, sprinkle
  with the seasoned bread crumbs, and drizzle with the melted
  butter.
♦ Put the lobsters into a roasting pan. Add ¼ inch water to the
  pan, cover the pan with aluminum foil, and bake 45 to 55
  minutes. When their backs are bright red, the lobsters are ready.

Wine recommendation: 1986 Latour Meursault (France)

POULTRY

Breast of Chicken, Lemon-Cream Sauce

*The chicken breasts can be
pounded with a wooden or
metal mallet made for the
purpose. The object is not to
pound the flesh thin, but to
break down the fibers in the
meat sufficiently to
accomplish two purposes:
one, to promote even
cooking, and, two, to
diminish shrinkage. Pound
each breast to roughly ½-inch
thickness.*

*Dust the breasts by dredging
them in the flour and shaking
off all excess. The light
coating of flour will help seal
in the chicken's juices.*

(MARINADE)
½ cup lemon juice
1 cup dry white wine
1 cup water
1 teaspoon salt
¼ teaspoon pepper
3 sprigs tarragon, chopped

1 small onion, minced
1 clove garlic, minced
4 6- to 8-ounce boned chicken
  breast halves, skinned and
  lightly pounded

(LEMON-CREAM SAUCE)
1 shallot, minced
2 ounces butter
¼ cup dry white wine
2 tablespoons lemon juice
1 sprig tarragon, chopped

4 sprigs thyme, chopped
1 pint heavy cream
¼ teaspoon salt
⅛ teaspoon white pepper

(TO COOK THE CHICKEN)

1 cup all-purpose flour
¼ teaspoon salt
¼ teaspoon pepper
¼ teaspoon ground sage

the chicken breasts
Lemon-Cream Sauce
¾ cup clarified butter

(MARINADE)

♦ In a blender, mix the lemon juice, white wine, water, salt, pepper, tarragon, onion, and garlic. Marinate the chicken breasts 24 hours in this mixture, turning the breasts occasionally.

(LEMON-CREAM SAUCE)

♦ Sauté the shallot in 1 ounce butter for 3 minutes. Add the white wine, lemon juice, tarragon, and thyme, and simmer until the liquid has almost all evaporated.
♦ Add the cream, and reduce by half. Season the sauce with the salt and pepper, and strain it.
♦ Return the sauce to the pan, and bring it back to a simmer. Work in 1 ounce butter until it is fully incorporated. Place the sauce in a holding container, cover it, and set it aside in a warm place.
♦ Preheat an oven to 325°F.

(TO COOK THE CHICKEN)

♦ Combine the flour with the salt, pepper, and sage. Remove the chicken breasts from the marinade, and pat them dry. Dust each chicken breast in the flour, and sauté it in the clarified butter until the breast is very lightly browned on both sides.
♦ Remove the breasts to a baking pan, and roast them at 325°F for 15 to 20 minutes, or until they are fully cooked.
♦ Remove the breasts to a platter or individual plates, and top them each with some of the Lemon-Cream Sauce. Serve them with Steamed Broccoli (page 68) and cellophane noodles (see glossary).

Wine recommendation: 1986 Lindeman's Padthanay Chardonnay (Australia) or William Hill Chardonnay (California)

Breast of Chicken, Apple-Chestnut Dressing

(APPLE-CHESTNUT DRESSING)

1½ cups white bread in ¼-inch cubes
1 Granny Smith apple, peeled, cored, and diced small
½ cup chestnuts, diced small

⅛ teaspoon ground sage
2 tablespoons applejack (apple brandy)
hot chicken stock to moisten (about ¼ cup)

To remove chestnuts from their shells, score an X on one side of each. Place the chestnuts on a pan in a preheated 375°F oven for 30 minutes. Remove the pan, and let the chestnuts cool. The shells will peel away easily.

(BEURRE BLANC)

2 shallots, minced

1 tablespoon white wine
  vinegar

¼ cup dry white wine

3 tablespoons dry vermouth

½ pound butter

(TO COOK THE CHICKEN)

4 8-ounce boneless chicken
  breast halves, with their skin

salt and white pepper

1 ounce melted butter

(APPLE-CHESTNUT DRESSING)

♦ Combine the cubed bread, diced apple, chestnuts, and sage in a
  bowl. Add the applejack. Add the chicken stock, and stir until
  all ingredients are moistened. Set the dressing aside.

(BEURRE BLANC)

♦ Combine the shallots, wine, and vermouth in a sauce pan. Simmer, and reduce by half.
♦ Add the butter in ½-inch pieces, and *montée*, or incorporate, it
  into the simmering wine.
♦ When the butter has been completely incorporated, remove the
  beurre blanc from the fire, pour it into a holding container, and
  place the container in a warm spot.

(TO COOK THE CHICKEN)

♦ Preheat the oven to 375°F.
♦ Lay the chicken breasts out, skin side down. Pound them gently
  with a mallet until they are about ⅓-inch thick. Sprinkle them
  with salt and pepper.
♦ Place a quarter of the dressing in the center of each breast. Fold
  the edges of the breast up around the stuffing, then invert the
  breast and place it in a baking dish. Repeat this procedure with
  the remaining three breasts.
♦ Brush the tops of the skin on all four breasts with melted butter.
♦ Roast the breasts 25 minutes, or until their skins are golden
  brown and crisp.
♦ Serve each breast with some of the *beurre blanc*, either under
  the breast or ladled over it.

Breast of Chicken, Côte D'Azur

(TO COOK THE CHICKEN)
½ cup flour
pinch each of salt and pepper
1 teaspoon minced fresh thyme
  leaves

4 8-ounce boned, skinned
  chicken breast halves, lightly
  pounded
½ cup olive oil

(TO COOK THE PEPPERS)
1 ounce butter
1 red bell pepper, diced
  medium

1 yellow bell pepper, diced
  medium
pinch each of salt and pepper

(SAUCE)
1 shallot, minced
1½ ounces butter
½ cup dry white wine

3 pinches saffron
2½ cups heavy cream
salt and pepper

(TO ASSEMBLE)
the chicken breasts
the peppers

the sauce

(TO COOK THE CHICKEN)
- Preheat an oven to 350°F.
- Combine the flour, salt, pepper, and thyme. Dust the chicken breasts lightly with the seasoned flour.
- Heat the olive oil in an ovenproof sauté pan or heavy skillet. Sauté the chicken breasts on both sides until light brown. Place the pan in the oven, and continue cooking for another 8 to 14 minutes.

(TO COOK THE PEPPERS)
- Sauté the diced peppers in the butter for 1 minute. Season with the salt and pepper. Set the peppers aside.

(SAUCE)
- Sauté the shallot in 1 ounce butter, covered, for 3 minutes. Add the white wine and saffron, and reduce by half.
- Add the heavy cream, and again reduce by half.
- Add ½ ounce butter in small pieces, and stir, while cooking, until the butter is fully incorporated. Season to taste with salt and pepper.

(TO ASSEMBLE)
- Place the chicken breasts on a serving platter or individual plates. Top each with some of the sauce, and sprinkle with the sautéed diced peppers. Serve.

1. Remove each drumstick by lifting it up with one hand, severing it from the thigh. Remove each thigh by pressing it outward and downward.

2. With a razor-sharp carving knife, slice the thighs and drumsticks lengthwise, removing the meat from around the bones.

3. Pull off the wings.

4. Make a horizontal incision through each breast at roughly the point where the wing was removed. Slice the breast vertically, as thin as possible, from the top, down to the horizontal incision. Continue until all the breast meat is sliced.

5. Once the meal is over, remove all remaining meat from the carcass. Use the leftovers in dishes such as hot and cold turkey sandwiches and cold turkey salad (the recipe for Pillar House Chicken Salad, pages 35–36, can serve as a guide), or along with the bones in soup stock.

Roast Turkey, Oyster-Chestnut Stuffing

(TURKEY STOCK)

giblets and neck from 1 10- to 12-pound turkey
1 medium Spanish onion, cut into eighths
1 carrot, with top removed, peeled and cut into ¼-inch rounds
1 stalk celery, cut crosswise into ¼-inch pieces

1 small leek, well rinsed and roughly cut
2 sprigs thyme
½ bunch parsley stems
1 bay leaf
½ teaspoon peppercorns, crushed

(OYSTER-CHESTNUT STUFFING)

½ pound butter
½ cup onion, diced medium
½ cup celery, diced medium
½ cup carrot, diced small
¼ cup fennel root, diced small
¼ teaspoon minced fresh sage leaves
¼ teaspoon fresh thyme leaves
¼ teaspoon minced fresh oregano leaves
½ pound fresh-ground, unseasoned pork sausage meat
2 large eggs

3 cups stale bread, cut or broken into ¼-inch pieces
¼ cup peeled, small-diced chestnuts
½ cup (about 16) shucked fresh oysters (see page 8)
1 tablespoon minced parsley
¼ teaspoon salt
¼ teaspoon white pepper
2 tablespoons Worcestershire sauce
about 1 cup strained turkey stock

(THE ROAST)

1 10- to 12-pound turkey
vegetable oil, salt, pepper, ground sage, and powdered thyme as needed
the remaining onion, carrot, celery, and leek
½ bunch parsley stems
2 sprigs thyme

1 bay leaf
½ teaspoon peppercorns, crushed
1 sprig rosemary
¼ cup flour
1 cup dry white wine
1 cup hot turkey stock
salt and pepper to taste

(TURKEY STOCK)

♦ Rinse the giblets and neck well in cold water. Place them in a stockpot with 1 gallon water, four of the onion pieces, half the carrot and celery slices, half the leek, the thyme, the parsley stems, the bay leaf, and the peppercorns (reserve the remaining vegetables to be roasted with the turkey). Simmer until the liquid is reduced by half.

(OYSTER-CHESTNUT STUFFING)
- ♦ Sauté in the butter the onion, celery, carrot, fennel, sage, thyme and oregano, covered, for 10 minutes. Remove the mixture from the fire, and set it aside.
- ♦ Sauté the ground sausage until it is fully cooked. Strain it, and discard the liquid.
- ♦ Put the diced bread into a large mixing bowl. Add the sautéed vegetables and herbs along with the chestnuts, oysters, sausage, eggs, parsley, salt, pepper, and Worcestershire sauce. Stir to blend well. Add enough strained turkey stock to fully moisten the stuffing. Set the stuffing aside, and allow it to cool.

(THE ROAST)
- ♦ Preheat an oven to 500°F.
- ♦ Rinse the turkey well, inside and out, with cold water. Pat it dry. Rub it inside and out with the vegetable oil, salt, pepper, sage, and thyme. Fill the turkey with the stuffing (be sure the stuffing has cooled first, or it may sour the turkey). Close the cavity with large bamboo skewers or small metal skewers.
- ♦ Place the bird in a large roasting pan, breast side up, and roast it 30 minutes. Turn the temperature down to 325°F, cover the turkey with aluminum foil, and continue roasting 1 hour. When the turkey is finished roasting, its internal temperature should be 160°F.
- ♦ Put the remaining cut onion, carrot, celery, and leek, along with the parsley stems, thyme, bay leaf, peppercorns, and rosemary, into the roasting pan with the turkey. Continue roasting until the turkey and vegetables are done; allow 16 minutes per pound total roasting time.
- ♦ Remove the pan from the oven, lift out the turkey, and set it aside. Place the roasting pan, with the remaining vegetables, herbs, fat, and juices, on top of the stove over a medium flame. Sprinkle in the flour, and blend well with a fork or whisk. Add the wine and 1 cup hot turkey stock. Blend well, and simmer until the gravy is thick and smooth. Thin the gravy, if desired, with additional stock.
- ♦ Strain the gravy into a holding container, and allow it to sit 15 minutes. Skim the fat from the top; discard the fat. Season the gravy to taste with salt and white pepper.
- ♦ Serve the sliced turkey, the stuffing, and the gravy, reheated, with Pillar House Whipped Potatoes (pages 70–71) and your choice of vegetable, salad, or both.

Ask a neighborhood butcher to bone, skin, and halve the duck breasts for you. The butcher can also remove the thigh portions from the birds, leaving the carcass, which you can use to make a rich stock for the sauce.

To prepare duck stock, follow the recipe for chicken stock, page 23; simply substitute duck bones for chicken bones. (If time does not allow you to prepare duck stock, you can substitute chicken stock.)

Roast Breast of Nantucket Duckling, Raspberry-Ginger Sauce

2 tablespoons vegetable oil
salt and white pepper
4 boned and skinned
    Nantucket (or other) duck
    breast halves
1 large shallot, minced
1 ounce butter
2 tablespoons brown sugar
2 tablespoons raspberry
    vinegar

¼ cup brandy
2 tablespoons Chambord
    liqueur
1½ cups duck stock
½ pint raspberries
1 bay leaf
1 sprig thyme, chopped
6 parsley stems, chopped
1 teaspoon grated fresh ginger

- Preheat an oven to 350°F.
- In a skillet or sauté pan, heat the vegetable oil.
- Lightly season the duck breasts with salt and pepper.
- Brown the breasts lightly on both sides. Roast them in the oven, in the same pan if it is ovenproof, for 8 to 10 minutes, or until they are medium rare.
- While the breasts roast, sauté the shallot in the butter, covered, over low heat for 5 minutes.
- Add the sugar, and lightly caramelize it.
- Add the raspberry vinegar, brandy, and Chambord. Add the duck stock, raspberries, and herbs. Reduce the sauce by a third, strain it, and press it through a fine sieve.
- Add the grated ginger.
- Slice each breast, on the bias, into 5 or 6 pieces. Place some sauce on a serving plate then arrange the duck pieces on the sauce.

Wine recommendation: 1986 McDowell Fumé Blanc (California)

Grilled Breast of Duckling, Mango-Port Sauce

(MANGO-PORT SAUCE)
1 ripe mango, peeled, pitted,
    and puréed in a food
    processor
1 shallot, minced
½ cup port wine

¼ teaspoon sugar
2 cups heavy cream
2 ounces butter
salt and white pepper

(TO GRILL THE DUCK)
4 boned duck breast halves
¼ cup vegetable oil

salt and white pepper
Mango-Port Sauce

(MANGO-PORT SAUCE)
- Combine the shallot and port wine in a sauce pan. Simmer, and reduce until nearly dry. Add the mango purée and sugar. Bring to a boil. Add the heavy cream. Simmer the sauce until it is reduced by half.
- Add the butter in ½-inch pieces, stirring them into the sauce until the butter is fully incorporated. Season the sauce to taste with salt and white pepper. Remove it to a holding container, and set it aside in a warm spot.

(TO GRILL THE DUCK)
- Preheat a broiler, or prepare an outdoor charcoal grill (see page 40).
- Brush the duck breasts with vegetable oil, and sprinkle them lightly with salt and pepper. Place the breasts on the grill or broiling pan, skin side down, and cook them 4 minutes. Turn them over, and continue cooking 5 or 6 minutes.
- Drain off excess fat, and place the breasts on an appropriate serving platter. Top them with the Mango-Port Sauce. Serve with Wild Rice Medley (page 69) and a fresh vegetable dish.

VEAL AND LAMB

Medallions of Veal, Ragout of Wild Mushrooms, and Marsala Cream

Other fresh mushrooms may be substituted for enokis, shitakes, chanterelles, and morels.

(MARSALA CREAM)
1 shallot, minced
1 ounce butter
1 cup dry marsala wine
1 teaspoon fresh thyme leaves

1 cup heavy cream
½ ounce unsalted butter
salt and pepper

(TO COOK THE VEAL)
8 3-ounce veal loin medallions, well trimmed

2 ounces butter
salt and pepper

(MUSHROOM RAGOUT)
1 ounce butter
½ cup enoki mushrooms
½ cup shitake mushrooms
½ cup chanterelle mushrooms
½ cup morel mushrooms

1 clove garlic, minced
½ teaspoon fresh thyme leaves
½ teaspoon fresh oregano leaves, minced

(MARSALA CREAM)

♦ Sauté the shallot in the butter, covered, for 5 minutes. Add the marsala and thyme, and reduce until only 2 tablespoons of liquid remain.

♦ Add the cream, and reduce by half. Pour the sauce into a blender, turn it on low speed, and add the butter. When the butter is fully incorporated, remove the sauce to a holding container. Season it to taste with salt and pepper, and place in a warm spot.

(TO COOK THE VEAL)

♦ Season the veal medallions with salt and pepper. Melt the butter in a skillet or sauté pan over a medium flame. Sauté the medallions 3 minutes on each side. Set them aside in a warm spot.

(MUSHROOM RAGOUT)

♦ Place 1 ounce of butter in a hot pan, add the mushrooms, and sauté them over high heat for 1 minute. Add the garlic, thyme, and oregano, and sauté 1 more minute.

♦ Remove the medallions to an appropriate serving platter. Top each medallion with a quarter of the mushroom ragout and some of the sauce.

Wine recommendation: 1986 Louis Michel Chablis, Premier Cru (France) or 1984 Beringer Cabernet Sauvignon (California)

Roulade of Veal, Garlic-Herb-Ricotta Stuffing

(VEAL DEMI-GLACE)

1 carrot with top removed, scrubbed and split lengthwise
1 Spanish onion, peeled and quartered
1 stalk celery, split lengthwise
1 small leek, well rinsed and split lengthwise
1 clove garlic, crushed
¼ cup vegetable oil

1 gallon brown stock of veal (page 24)
1 bunch parsley stems, tied together with string
4 sprigs thyme
2 bay leaves
1 teaspoon black peppercorns, crushed
optional: ¼ teaspoon salt

(VEAL SUPREME SAUCE)

2 tablespoons clarified butter
1 shallot, minced
¼ cup brandy
4 sprigs thyme, chopped

6 stems parsley, chopped
1 bay leaf
¾ cup veal *demi-glace*
1 pint heavy cream

(GARLIC-HERB-RICOTTA STUFFING)

1½ cups ricotta cheese
1 small round Boursin cheese
1 clove garlic, minced
1 teaspoon minced fresh basil
   leaves
1 teaspoon chopped fresh
   thyme

½ teaspoon dried oregano
¼ cup seasoned dry bread
   crumbs (page 39)
salt and pepper

(TO ASSEMBLE)

8 veal medallions or cutlets,
   about 2½ ounces each (or
   1¼ pounds total), pounded
   ⅛-inch thick
4 teaspoons dijon mustard

Garlic-Herb-Ricotta Stuffing
½ cup vegetable oil
½ cup flour
Veal Supreme Sauce

(VEAL DEMI-GLACE)

- Bring the stock to a simmer; skim.
- Place the carrot, onion, celery, leek, and garlic in a 2-gallon stockpot with the vegetable oil. Sauté the vegetables 15 to 20 minutes, or until they are well caramelized.
- Add the stock and remaining ingredients. Simmer 1 to 2 hours, until the stock is reduced by half.
- Strain the stock and discard the aromatics. Return the stock to the fire in a smaller pot. Simmer until the stock is again reduced by half.
- Strain the stock again into a smaller sauce pan. Continue reducing until it is thick and rich.
- Strain, cool, cover, and refrigerate the *demi-glace* until you are ready to use it.

(VEAL SUPREME SAUCE)

- Sauté the shallot in the butter, covered, for 1 minute. Add the brandy and ignite. Simmer until reduced by half.
- Add the thyme, parsley stems, bay leaf, and veal *demi-glace*, and reduce to a quarter of the original volume.
- Add the heavy cream, and reduce by half. Strain the sauce, pour it into an appropriate holding container, and cover it. Set it aside in a warm spot.

(GARLIC-HERB-RICOTTA STUFFING)

- Combine the ricotta cheese, Boursin cheese, garlic, basil, thyme, oregano, bread crumbs, and salt and pepper to taste in a mixing bowl. Stir until well blended.

(TO ASSEMBLE)

- Lay the medallions on a clean surface. Spread each with a thin coating of mustard (about ½ teaspoon). Spoon a tablespoon of

Traditional French cooking recognizes five basic "mother sauces": espagnole, velouté, béchamel, hollandaise, and tomato (respectively, brown, blond, white, dutch, and tomato).

Traditional demi-glace was derived from espagnole, brown sauce, which is thickened with a roux, a mixture of flour and fat. Demi-glace was made by combining one part espagnole, and one part brown stock, plus an assortment of aromatics, and reducing them by half (from this half reduction comes the French name; demi means "half").

As the gastronomic community has responded to the current demand for honest and wholesome foods, flour, once used to thicken many sauces, has often been removed. Its place has been taken by natural reductions, of which our demi-glace is an example. The thickness of our demi-glace is derived from elements infused into the original brown stock, supplemented by the aromatics called for here and concentrated by repeated reductions.

Boursin is a brand name for a soft garlic- and herb-flavored cheese, very similar to cream cheese. If Boursin is unavailable, you can substitute a similar brand. Or use an equal amount of cream cheese and lightly increase the quantities of aromatic ingredients called for.

the stuffing down the center of each medallion. Roll the medallion around the stuffing, and secure it with a round wooden toothpick.

♦ Preheat an oven to 350°F.

♦ Pour the oil into an iron skillet or ovenproof sauté pan, and set the pan over a medium fire. Dust the medallions with flour, and place them in the hot oil, their toothpick-sealed edges up. Sauté the medallions until they are golden brown on the outside. Continue cooking them in the oven for 5 minutes, or until they are done.

♦ Drain off excess oil, remove the toothpicks, and place the medallions on individual plates or on a platter. Top each with some of the heated Veal Supreme Sauce, and serve.

Veal Sauté, Crab and Tarragon Sauce

(CRAB AND TARRAGON SAUCE)

1 ounce butter
1 shallot, minced
1 teaspoon minced fresh
   tarragon leaves
2 tablespoons tarragon-
   flavored vinegar

¼ cup dry white wine
1½ cups heavy cream
½ cup cooked fresh Maine (or
   other) crab meat
salt and white pepper

(TO COOK THE VEAL)

4 6-ounce (or 8 3-ounce) veal
   cutlets
½ cup flour
¼ teaspoon each of salt, white
   pepper, and minced fresh
   thyme, tarragon, and
   oregano leaves

½ cup olive oil
Crab and Tarragon Sauce

(CRAB AND TARRAGON SAUCE)

♦ Sauté the shallot in the butter, covered, for 3 minutes.

♦ Add the tarragon, vinegar, and white wine, and reduce by half.

♦ Add the heavy cream, and again reduce by half.

♦ Add the crab meat, and season it to taste with salt and pepper. Set the sauce aside, and keep it warm.

(TO COOK THE VEAL)

♦ Combine the flour, salt, pepper, thyme, tarragon, and oregano. Dust the veal cutlets lightly in the seasoned flour.

♦ Heat the oil in a sauté pan or skillet. Cook the cutlets on both sides until they are done. Place them on individual plates or on an appropriate platter, and top them with the Crab and Tarragon Sauce.

Roast Rack of Lamb, Rosemary-Pommery Sauce

(ROSEMARY-POMMERY SAUCE)
1 ounce butter
1 shallot, minced
½ cup petit sirah or other
  light-bodied red wine
4 sprigs fresh rosemary,
  chopped

1 sprig fresh thyme, chopped
1 bay leaf
1 pint heavy cream
3 teaspoons Pommery mustard
salt and pepper

(TO ROAST THE LAMB)
2 whole racks of spring lamb,
  split, with chine bone
  removed, trimmed, and
  frenched
4 teaspoons dijon mustard

2 teaspoons minced fresh
  rosemary
salt and pepper
¼ cup vegetable oil
Rosemary-Pommery Sauce

(ROSEMARY-POMMERY SAUCE)
- Sauté the shallot in the butter, covered, for 3 minutes. Add the wine, rosemary, thyme, and bay leaf. Reduce until almost dry.
- Add the cream, and reduce by half. Strain the sauce.
- Bring the sauce back to a simmer, add the mustard, and season to taste with the salt and pepper. Remove the sauce to a holding container, cover it, and place it in a warm spot.

(TO ROAST THE LAMB)
- Preheat an oven to 450°F.
- Spread each half rack with a teaspoon of mustard. Sprinkle with the rosemary, salt, and pepper.
- Heat the oil in a skillet or sauté pan. Place the racks in this pan, concave side up. When they are lightly browned, remove them to a roasting pan. Roast to the desired degree of doneness.
- To serve, cut each rack into 4 chops, with 2 bones per chop. Ladle some of the Rosemary-Pommery Sauce onto an individual plate. Arrange the four double chops in the center of the plate, the bones crossed. Garnish with a sprig of fresh rosemary.

Wine recommendation: 1985 Charton of Trebucket Bourgogne Pinot Noir (France)

The rack of a lamb is the lower portion of the rib cage. When it is split, it will produce two half racks (but one of these halves, as ordered in a restaurant, is referred to as a rack of lamb).

Have your butcher prepare the rack as specified. The chine bone, or backbone, must be removed before the rack can be cut into individual chops. To french the rack is to remove the meat that interconnects the rib bones (you might add this meat to a lamb stew or curry), and with a small knife, to scrape each bone to remove all sinew, skin, and fat. This step adds finesse to the final presentation. The rack is then trimmed of the fat attached to the loin, which has no use in this dish.

Most lamb lovers prefer the meat cooked medium-rare. At a temperature of 450°F, 15 minutes' roasting time will produce rare, 20 to 25 minutes' medium-rare, 35 minutes' medium, and 45 minutes' well-done meat.

BEEF

Sirloin Steak, Roquefort Sauce

Prime is the highest of the
seven U.S. Department of
Agriculture grades of beef.
Prime beef is well marbled—
that is, fat is evenly
distributed through it, giving
it exceptional flavor and
above-average tenderness. The
other grades of beef, from
better to worse, are choice,
good, commercial, standard,
cutter, and canner. The lower
the grade, the less marbling
present. If prime beef is
unavailable, ask for choice.

Roquefort cheese is produced
in the French town by the
same name. A mold,
introduced into the milk and
cream at a certain point in the
creation of this cheese,
produces the blue veins for
which it is well known. If
Roquefort is unavailable,
substitute another good blue
cheese such as Gorgonzola,
Danish Blue, or Oregon Blue.

(ROQUEFORT SAUCE)

2 cups heavy cream

3 tablespoons crumbled
  Roquefort cheese

pinch salt

(TO PREPARE THE STEAKS)

4 13-ounce prime, aged,
  boneless sirloin steaks,
  trimmed of excess fat

salt and pepper

2 teaspoons vegetable oil
1 bunch watercress
Roquefort Sauce

(ROQUEFORT SAUCE)

♦ Bring the cream to a boil, and simmer until it is reduced by half.
  Add the Roquefort cheese and salt, and set aside.

(TO PREPARE THE STEAKS)

♦ Preheat a broiler.
♦ Brush both sides of each steak with vegetable oil, and season
  both sides lightly with salt and pepper. Place the steaks on a
  baking sheet or roasting pan, and broil one side, then the other,
  to the desired degree of doneness (6 to 7 minutes per side for
  rare, 8 to 10 minutes per side for medium-rare, and 12 minutes
  per side for well-done).
♦ Garnish each steak with a small bunch of watercress, and serve
  the Roquefort Sauce on the side.

Wine recommendation: 1983 Louis Jadot Beaune Bressandes (France)

Filet Mignon, Zinfandel-Morel Sauce

If morel mushrooms are
unavailable fresh, substitute
the dried version. At least 5
hours ahead, rinse the dried
mushrooms well in cold
water. Immerse them first in
water for 1 hour, then in the
½ cup zinfandel wine for 3 to
4 hours. Use this wine in the
sauce according to the recipe.
  If you would prefer to use
fresh mushrooms, you might
substitute shitakes, oyster
mushrooms, or chanterelles.

Zinfandel, a robust red wine,
is made only in California.

(ZINFANDEL-MOREL SAUCE)

1 small Spanish onion, minced
1 stalk celery, minced
1 small carrot, peeled and
  minced
1 leek, white part only, well
  rinsed and minced
1 shallot, minced
1 ounce butter
1 clove garlic, minced
1 sprig fresh thyme, chopped

3 sprigs fresh oregano,
  chopped
1 bay leaf
½ cup zinfandel wine
1½ cups *demi-glace* (page 55),
  made with veal or beef stock
1 cup morel mushrooms
1 teaspoon butter
salt and pepper

(TO PREPARE THE STEAKS)

4 8-ounce beef tenderloin steaks, fully trimmed	½ teaspoon salt
1 teaspoon pepper	¼ cup vegetable oil

(ZINFANDEL-MOREL SAUCE)

♦ Sauté the onion, celery, carrot, leek, and shallot in the butter until the vegetables are caramelized.
♦ Add the garlic and herbs, and sauté another minute.
♦ Add the zinfandel, and reduce until nearly dry.
♦ Add the *demi-glace*, and simmer 10 minutes. Strain the sauce, then season it to taste with salt and pepper. Add the morels, and *montée* the butter over the fire. Remove the sauce to a holding container, cover it, and set it aside.

(TO PREPARE THE STEAKS)

♦ Preheat an oven to 425°F.
♦ Vigorously rub salt and pepper into the steaks.
♦ Heat the oil in a skillet or sauté pan. Brown the steaks well, about 2 minutes on each side. Remove them to a baking pan or baking sheet, and roast them at 375°F to desired doneness (6 minutes for rare, 8 to 10 minutes for medium-rare, and 15 minutes for well-done meat).
♦ Serve the sauce on the side.

Roast Angus Prime Rib au Jus

(JUS)

2 pounds beef marrow bones, 2 to 3 inches long	5 overripe tomatoes, stem end removed
2 tablespoons salt	¼ cup vegetable oil
1 large Spanish onion, peeled and cut into eighths	4 parsley stems
2 celery stalks, roughly cut	4 sprigs thyme
2 carrots, peeled and roughly cut	4 fresh basil leaves
	1 bay leaf

(TO PREPARE THE ROAST)

1 9- to 10-pound rib roast, oven-ready (trimmed and tied)	salt and pepper
	the *jus*

(JUS)

♦ Place the marrow bones and salt in a stockpot with 1 gallon cold water. Bring the water to a boil, skim and discard excess fat from the top, then drain off and discard the water.
♦ Preheat an oven to 400°F.
♦ Add 1¼ gallons fresh water to the bones in the stockpot, and

A thermometer can be of tremendous value in determining when roast meat is done. Slide the thermometer into the center of the roast. Remove the roast from the oven when its internal temperature is 15 to 20 degrees below the desired final temperature; it will continue to cook in its stored heat. The roast is ready to serve at these final temperatures: rare, 140°F; medium, 150°F; well-done, 160°F.

When meat is roasted, its juices tend to move away from the source of heat—that is, they move toward the middle of the roast. The final 15-minute resting period allows the juices to be redistributed throughout the roast.

bring the water to a simmer. Skim off any impurities that collect at the top.

♦ Place the onion, celery, carrots, tomatoes, and vegetable oil in a roasting pan. Roast in the oven, stirring every 10 to 15 minutes, until all ingredients are very well caramelized (dark brown).

♦ Skim the stock again, then add the roasted aromatics. Add the parsley, thyme, basil, and bay leaf. Continue simmering 3 to 4 hours, till the stock is reduced by about a quart.

♦ Strain the stock, and return it to the fire. Continue simmering, skimming periodically, until the stock is reduced by half, yielding about ½ gallon of rich, clear broth.

(TO PREPARE THE ROAST)
♦ Preheat an oven to 500°F.
♦ Season the rib generously with salt and pepper.
♦ Place the rib in a roasting pan, fat side up. Put the pan into the 500°F oven for 30 minutes. Turn the oven temperature down to 425°F, and continue roasting to the desired degree of doneness (20 minutes for rare, 40 minutes for medium-rare, 60 minutes for well-done meat).
♦ When the roasting period is completed, turn the oven off and leave the roast in the oven for 15 minutes. Remove it from the oven, and allow it to rest in a warm spot for 15 more minutes.
♦ Cut the string from the roast, and remove the outer fat layer. Carve the roast, and serve it with the hot *jus*.

Wine recommendation: 1984 Château Montelena Cabernet (France)

Chateaubriand,
Bouquet of Seasonal Vegetables

Feel free to substitute other vegetables, depending on the season and your region. During the warm summer months, farmers throughout New England set up small produce stands; snap beans, zucchini, corn, and cauliflower are among the offerings you could use in this dish. In autumn, you might include butternut squash, acorn squash, or even sweet potatoes.

(TO PREPARE THE POTATOES AND TOMATOES)

3 very large all-purpose potatoes	1 tablespoon seasoned dry bread crumbs (page 39)
4 small tomatoes	1 ounce melted butter
1 tablespoon fresh-grated parmesan cheese	¼ cup vegetable oil

(TO ROAST THE BEEF)

¼ cup vegetable oil	2 cloves garlic, minced
1 2½-pound tenderloin roast, trimmed and tied	salt and pepper

(TO ROAST THE VEGETABLES)

12 thick asparagus stalks, peeled and trimmed to 5 inches long

1 large yellow crookneck squash, cut into 2-inch julienne

4 large broccoli flowerettes, from 1 or 2 stems

12 baby carrots, with tops removed, peeled and cut into 1-inch lengths

2 ounces butter

salt and pepper

(TO PREPARE THE POTATOES AND TOMATOES)

♦ Preheat an oven to 425°F.

♦ Quarter the potatoes by cutting each in half crosswise, then cutting the halves lengthwise. With a sharp paring knife shape, or "turn," each quarter into an olive or football shape. Immerse the pieces in cold water.

♦ Remove a very thin slice of tomato from the bottom of each tomato (to keep it from rolling around). Remove a slice from the top of the tomato, about ¼-inch thick. With the point of the knife, cut out whatever remains of the tomato core. Combine the grated parmesan and the seasoned bread crumbs, and sprinkle some of the mixture on top of each tomato. Top this with a drizzle of melted butter. Remove the tomatoes to a baking pan, and set the pan aside.

♦ Heat an ovenproof skillet or sauté pan with ¼ cup vegetable oil. Remove the potatoes from the water, pat them *very* dry, and put them into the hot oil in the pan. Brown them lightly on all sides. Season them lightly with salt and pepper. Set the pan aside.

(TO ROAST THE BEEF)

♦ Heat a large skillet or sauté pan with ¼ cup vegetable oil. Rub the garlic, salt, and pepper vigorously into the meat.

♦ Brown the filet well on all sides. Remove it to a roasting pan, and roast 30 minutes for rare, 35 minutes for medium-rare, or 45 minutes for well-done meat.

(TO ROAST THE VEGETABLES)

♦ Thirty minutes before the roast is done, set the pan containing the potatoes in the oven.

♦ While the meat and potatoes cook, steam, or blanch in boiling salted water, the asparagus, squash, broccoli, and baby carrots, each separately, until al dente.

♦ Ten minutes before the roast is done, put the baking pan with the four tomatoes into the oven. Remove it after 10 minutes, along with the roast and the potatoes. Place the roast on a platter.

♦ Briefly sauté the asparagus, squash, broccoli, and baby carrots,

Turning, from the French tourner, is a technique of shaping a vegetable into an olive or football shape by taking a "turn" around it with a sharp paring knife. This is part of the craft that transforms ordinary fare into extraordinary cuisine.

There are two reasons to dry the turned potatoes well: one, to prevent the oil from splattering when you put them into the hot pan, and, two, to prevent them from sticking to the pan.

each separately, in the butter, and season with salt and pepper. Arrange all the vegetables around the roast, and serve.

Wine recommendation: 1979 Château Lynch-Bages Bordeaux (France)

Broiled Tips of Tenderloin

1 large egg
¼ teaspoon fresh thyme leaves
¼ teaspoon minced fresh sage leaves
¼ teaspoon minced fresh coriander leaves
1 large clove garlic, crushed
¼ teaspoon salt
¼ teaspoon white pepper
½ cup olive oil
2 teaspoons rice vinegar

2 tablespoons sake (Japanese rice wine)
1½ pounds beef tenderloin, trimmed of fat and sinew and cut into 24 1-inch pieces
salt and pepper
1 small Spanish onion
1 small red or yellow bell pepper
4 cherry tomatoes

♦ Cut the onion and pepper lengthwise into quarters. Cut each quarter in half crosswise. Remove the ribs and seeds from the pepper pieces.
♦ Place the egg, herbs, garlic, salt, and pepper in a blender. Turn the blender on low speed, and pour in the olive oil in a slow, steady stream. Alternate with the vinegar and sake. If the marinade becomes too thick, thin it with water, a teaspoon at a time.
♦ Preheat a broiler.
♦ Season the meat with salt and pepper. Push the meat, onion, and pepper pieces alternately onto four metal skewers. Put a cherry tomato at the end of each skewer.
♦ Brush the meat and vegetables with some of the marinade. Broil for approximately 10 minutes, turning each skewer 3 or 4 times during the cooking.

Filet Mignon Rossini

(MADEIRA SAUCE)
¼ cup each of minced onion, celery, carrot, and leek
1 ounce butter
1 shallot, minced
1 bay leaf
2 sprigs fresh thyme

6 parsley stems
½ cup madeira wine
1½ cups veal *demi-glace* (page 55)
salt and pepper

(TO PREPARE THE MEAT)

8 4-ounce beef tenderloin medallions, well trimmed
salt and pepper
¼ cup olive oil

8 ½-ounce slices of fresh grade-A *foie gras* (goose liver)
Madeira Sauce

(MADEIRA SAUCE)

- Sauté the chopped vegetables in the butter, and caramelize them well. Add the bay leaf, thyme, and parsley. Add the madeira wine, and reduce by half.
- Add the veal *demi-glace*. Simmer, and reduce by one-quarter. Season to taste with salt and pepper. Strain the sauce, remove it to a holding container, and set the container aside in a warm spot.

(TO PREPARE THE MEAT)

- Sprinkle the beef medallions lightly with salt and pepper. In a sauté pan, sauté them 2 to 3 minutes on each side in olive oil.
- Remove the medallions to a platter, and keep them warm. Gently sauté the goose liver slices in the same pan the meat was sautéed in. Top each medallion with a slice of the sautéed goose liver. Top the meat with some of the Madeira Sauce, and serve.

Foie gras, *("fat liver")* comes from geese raised specifically for the high fat content of their livers. An American version of foie gras *has been developed recently; one producer is in New York state. If you are unable to find fresh* foie gras, *you may wish to substitute canned goose liver "mousse," which can be found in most gourmet markets.*

Filet Mignon, Four Peppercorn Sauce

(FOUR PEPPERCORN SAUCE)

1 tablespoon white peppercorns, crushed
1 tablespoon black peppercorns, crushed
1 tablespoon green peppercorns
1 tablespoon pink peppercorns

1 ounce butter
2 shallots, minced
½ cup veal *demi-glace* (page 55)
2 cups heavy cream
salt

(TO PREPARE THE BEEF)

8 4-ounce beef tenderloin medallions
salt, black pepper, and vegetable oil as needed

Four Peppercorn Sauce

(FOUR PEPPERCORN SAUCE)

- Sauté the peppercorns and shallots covered, in the butter. Add the *demi-glace*, and reduce by half. Add the heavy cream, and reduce by half again. Season as needed with salt.

(TO PREPARE THE BEEF)

- Lightly sprinkle the beef medallions with salt and pepper. Sauté them 2 to 3 minutes on each side in vegetable oil. Top each medallion with some of the Four Peppercorn Sauce, and serve.

MISCELLANEOUS

Sautéed Calves' Liver with Onion and Bacon

*We recommend you use only
fresh calves' liver for this
recipe. Calves' liver is
superior to beef liver in both
flavor and tenderness.*

8 thick slices bacon
1 large Spanish onion, peeled
    and cut into ⅛-inch slices
salt and pepper
½ cup vegetable oil
1½ pounds fresh prime calves'
    liver, trimmed and cut into 8
    thin slices

½ cup flour
¼ teaspoon each of salt, white
    pepper, and paprika

♦ In a cast-iron skillet, fry the bacon slices until they are brown
  and crisp. Remove them to absorbent paper to drain.
♦ In the same skillet, sauté the onions in ¼ cup vegetable oil, until
  they are lightly browned. Season them with salt and pepper.
  Remove them with a slotted spoon, and set them aside.
♦ Add the remaining ¼ cup oil to the same skillet. Combine the
  flour with the salt, white pepper, and paprika, and dust the liver
  slices with the mixture. When the pan is *very hot*, add the liver,
  and sauté it 2 minutes on each side. Remove it to a platter.
♦ Put the onions back into the pan. When they are hot, arrange
  them on top of the liver. Top each portion with two crossed
  bacon slices, and serve.

Seafood Omelette

*If you buy any of the seafood
raw, cook it as you prefer.
You can sauté the diced
swordfish and scallops in
butter, or poach them in
butter and a little dry white
wine. Titi shrimp, the very
tiny ones, are always sold
cooked. Lobster meat can
also be purchased cooked.*

(LOBSTER SAUCE)
½ small carrot, peeled and
    minced
½ small Spanish onion, minced
½ stalk celery, minced
1 shallot, minced
2 ounces butter
½ teaspoon flour
½ teaspoon paprika
1 sprig fresh thyme, chopped
¼ cup dry sherry
¼ cup brandy

1 pint lobster stock (page 25)
1½ cups heavy cream
½ cup cooked and medium-
    diced lobster meat
½ cup cooked and quartered
    bay scallops
½ cup cooked and medium-
    diced swordfish
½ cup titi shrimp (see page 7)
salt and pepper

(OMELETTE)
12 large eggs
½ cup light cream or half and
    half
½ teaspoon fresh thyme leaves
¼ teaspoon salt

¼ teaspoon pepper
3 ounces clarified butter (see
    page 28)
the remaining seafood
Lobster Sauce

(LOBSTER SAUCE)

♦ Sauté the carrot, onion, celery, and shallot in 2 ounces butter for 5 minutes. Stir in the flour and paprika, and cook 1 minute. Add the thyme.

♦ Add the sherry and brandy, and reduce until almost dry. Add the lobster stock; simmer, and reduce by half. Add the cream, and reduce again by half.

♦ Stir together all the cooked seafood.

♦ Strain the sauce, add to it half the seafood, and season it to taste with salt and pepper. Remove the sauce to a holding container, cover it, and set it aside in a warm place.

(OMELETTE)

♦ Crack the eggs into a large mixing bowl or blender. Add the light cream, thyme, salt, and pepper, and beat well.

♦ Heat 1 ounce of the butter in an 8-inch non-stick pan. Place one-quarter of the remaining seafood in the pan. When the butter and seafood are hot, pour in one-quarter of the egg, cream, and thyme mixture. Over a medium flame, stir this mixture as if you were making scrambled eggs. When the eggs have just begun to set, lift the pan a few inches from the fire, and tip it down and away from you at roughly a 30-degree angle. Then, with a wooden spoon or rubber spatula, gently but briskly flip the outer edge of the egg mass into itself, bit by bit. Continue until the omelette is completely rolled up, sitting in the side of the pan away from you. Set the pan down again over the medium fire, and allow the omelette to become very lightly browned.

♦ Lift and tilt the pan again, rolling the omelette out onto a serving plate. Top it with some of the Lobster Sauce, and serve.

♦ Repeat the last two steps three times with the remaining egg mixture, seafood, and Lobster Sauce.

The etymology of the word omelette is uncertain. According to Larousse Gastronomique *(no relation to David Paul), omelette may be a corruption of the French word amelette, "blade," derived from another French word, alumette, "matchstick."*

That an omelette is shaped rather like a knife blade gives credence to this theory. Another theory says omelette is derived from ova mellita or ovemele, a dish of eggs and honey. A recipe for this dish was written by the Roman gourmand Apicius, 342 to 410 A.D.

"An omelette is to haute cuisine what the sonnet is to poetry."—Alexander Dumas

*"The theory of preparing an omelette is at once simple and complicated."—*The Art of French Cooking

"By now I know, fatalistically, that if I am using a pan I know, and if I have properly rolled the precise amount of sweet butter around that pan, and if the stars, winds, and general emotional climates are in both conjunction and harmony, I can make a perfect omelette without ever touching a spatula to it."—M. F. K. Fisher

*To make your own fettuccine,
see pages 18–19.*

Fettuccine with Fresh Herbs and Vegetables

(TO COOK THE FETTUCCINE)
1 teaspoon salt
3 tablespoons olive oil
1 pound fresh fettuccine (half
  saffron and half spinach, if
  available)

½ ounce butter

(SAUCE)
2 ounces butter
½ cup carrot, in 1-by-⅛-⅛-
  inch julienne
½ cup broccoli flowerettes
½ cup yellow crookneck
  squash, sliced ¼-inch thick
½ cup zucchini, in 1-by-¼-by-
  ¼-inch julienne
1 red bell pepper, seeds and
  ribs removed, in 1-by-⅛-by-
  ⅛-inch julienne

2 cloves garlic, minced
½ teaspoon fresh thyme leaves
1 teaspoon minced fresh basil
  leaves
2 teaspoons minced parsley
¼ teaspoon salt
¼ teaspoon pepper
½ cup dry white wine

(TO ASSEMBLE)
the vegetable mixture
the cooked fettuccine

¼ cup fresh-grated parmesan
  cheese

(TO COOK THE FETTUCCINE)
♦ Add the salt and olive oil to a stockpot with 2 gallons water,
  and bring the water to a rapid boil. Drop in the fettuccine, and
  stir, separating the strands, until the water returns to a rapid
  boil. Boil the pasta 1 minute, then drain it. Remove it to a large
  bowl, toss it with the butter, and set it aside.

(THE SAUCE)
♦ Melt the butter in a large sauté pan. Add the carrots, and sauté
  them 4 minutes. Add the remaining vegetables: broccoli, yellow
  squash, zucchini, red pepper, and garlic. Sauté them 2 minutes,
  coating all the vegetables well with the butter. Add the herbs,
  salt, pepper, and wine. Cover, and simmer 5 minutes.

(TO ASSEMBLE)
♦ Add the vegetable mixture to the large bowl holding the pasta.
  Add the grated parmesan, and toss all. Serve on individual plates
  or one large platter.

5 · Accompaniments

Grilled Eggplant

1 large eggplant, sliced into 1-inch-thick rounds
salt
2 peeled, seeded and medium-diced tomatoes (tomato fondue, page 19)

2 cloves garlic, minced
¼ teaspoon each of minced fresh thyme, basil, and oregano leaves
about ½ cup olive oil
¼ cup grated parmesan cheese

The salt draws some of the water from the eggplant and reduces the vegetable's acidity.

♦ Prepare an outdoor grill, or preheat a broiler.
♦ Sprinkle the sliced eggplant on both sides with salt. Place the slices in a colander or strainer, and allow them to sit 1 hour.
♦ Sauté the tomatoes, herbs, and garlic in ¼ cup olive oil for 2 minutes. Set the pan aside.
♦ Brush the eggplant slices on both sides with olive oil. Grill or broil them, turning once, until both sides are golden brown.
♦ Place the eggplant slices on a serving platter. Top them with the garlic, tomato, and herbs, and sprinkle parmesan cheese over.

Roasted Leeks and Celeriac with Walnuts

¼ cup olive oil
4 small leeks, split in half lengthwise to within an inch of the base, well washed, dark outer leaves removed
1 small celeriac (celery root) peeled and sliced ¼-inch thick

½ cup shelled walnut halves, cut in half lengthwise
1 teaspoon grated fresh ginger
¼ cup chopped fresh coriander
1 clove garlic, minced
¼ teaspoon salt
¼ teaspoon white pepper

♦ Preheat an oven to 400°F.
♦ Pour the olive oil into a roasting pan, and set the pan in the preheated oven for 5 minutes. Place the leeks and celeriac in the hot pan, and roast 10 minutes, stirring occasionally.

◆ Add the remaining ingredients, stir well, and cover. Roast 15 to 20 minutes more, or until the vegetables are soft.

Steamed Broccoli

1 bunch broccoli

◆ Cut up the broccoli, leaving 1 to 3 inches of stem connected to each flowerette. Peel the rest of the stems, and slice them to be cooked along with the flowerettes (or reserve them for cream of broccoli soup or an Asian-style stir-fry). Split the flowerettes into halves, thirds, or quarters, as you prefer.
◆ Bring 1 inch of water in a sauce pan to a boil. Place a steaming basket in the pan, and add the broccoli. Cook the broccoli 5 to 6 minutes, until al dente.
◆ Serve with melted butter and fresh lemon juice or the sauce of your choice.

Steaming vegetables preserves nutrients that would be released into the water were the vegetables boiled.

Be careful not to steam the broccoli too long. Since steam is hotter than boiling water, steamed vegetables cook a little faster than their boiled counterparts.

Asparagus, Sauce Vergé

1½ pounds asparagus	juice of ½ lemon
½ cup *crème fraiche* (page 12)	2 tablespoons minced chives
2 tablespoons dijon mustard	

◆ Cut off and discard the woody end of each asparagus spear. Peel each spear, using a vegetable peeler.
◆ Combine the *crème fraiche*, mustard, and lemon juice in a small sauce pan. Place the pan over medium heat, and stir frequently until the sauce is hot. Add the chives. Set the sauce aside until you are ready to use it.
◆ Put the asparagus spears into boiling salted water, and simmer approximately 3 minutes. Drain, pat the spears dry, and transfer them to a platter. Top with the sauce, or serve it on the side.

Peel each spear carefully to avoid breaking it. Though peeling asparagus may seem wasteful, you need remove only a very thin layer. Cooking peeled asparagus reveals graduated shades of green, greatly intensifying the vegetable's regal appearance. And you can use the peelings, along with the woody ends, to make creamed asparagus soup. Garnish the soup with diced spears.

Sautéed Yellow Squash, Bell Pepper, and Eggplant

1 red bell pepper	1 clove garlic, minced
1 yellow bell pepper	2 tablespoons minced fresh
1 yellow squash	basil leaves
1 small eggplant, peeled	1 teaspoon minced fresh
juice of 1 lemon	oregano leaves
¼ cup olive oil	salt and pepper

◆ Cut the peppers and squash into large julienne strips (¼ inch by ¼ inch by 2 inches). Cut the eggplant into very large julienne (½ inch by ½ inch by 2½ inches). Rinse the eggplant sticks in a pint of water mixed with the lemon juice to prevent them from turning brown.

♦ Heat the oil in a sauté pan. Add the pepper strips and garlic, and sauté 2 minutes. Add the squash, and sauté another minute. Add the eggplant and herbs, and salt and pepper to taste. Sauté another 3 to 5 minutes, or until the vegetables are cooked to your preference. Adjust the seasonings as needed.

Rice Pilaf

1 medium Spanish onion, diced small
1 ounce butter
1 cup long-grained white rice
1 bay leaf

pinch each of salt and white pepper
2 cups white stock of chicken (page 23)

♦ Sauté the onion in the butter, covered, for 5 minutes.
♦ Preheat an oven to 350°F.
♦ Add the rice and the bay leaf to the onion and the butter. Sauté 3 minutes, stirring the rice well to coat it with the butter.
♦ Add the salt, pepper, and chicken stock. Stir, blending all ingredients well. Bring the stock to a boil, cover the pan, and put it in the oven. Bake 20 minutes. Remove the pan from the oven, and serve.

Wild Rice Medley

½ cup wild rice
3 cups water
pinch salt
½ cup small-diced scallions
1½ ounces butter
1 clove garlic, minced

1 cup button mushrooms, quartered
1 cup fresh-cooked Rice Pilaf (page 69)
pinch each of salt and pepper

♦ Boil the wild rice in the salted water about 30 minutes, until it is tender and fully cooked. Drain, and set the wild rice aside.
♦ Sauté the scallion in the butter for 3 minutes. Add the garlic and the mushrooms, and sauté another 3 minutes.
♦ Add the rice pilaf and the wild rice. Season with salt and pepper.

Brown Rice with Spicy Pecans

(TO PREPARE THE PECANS)
1 cup whole shelled pecans
2 tablespoons olive oil
½ teaspoon Old Bay Seafood Seasoning

6 dashes Tabasco sauce
1 clove garlic, minced

(TO COOK THE RICE)

1 cup long-grained brown rice	1 tablespoon dijon mustard
1½ cups water	¼ cup minced parsley
¼ teaspoon salt	¼ teaspoon salt
1 medium Spanish onion, diced medium	¼ teaspoon pepper
¼ cup olive oil	the spiced pecans
1 clove garlic, minced	
½ cup peeled, seeded, and medium-diced tomatoes (tomato fondue, page 19)	

(TO PREPARE THE PECANS)

♦ Preheat an oven to 375°F.
♦ Combine the pecans, oil, Old Bay Seasoning, Tabasco, and garlic, and spread the mixture in a casserole dish. Bake 20 minutes. Remove the dish from the oven, and set it aside.

(TO COOK THE RICE)

♦ Rinse the brown rice very well in several changes of cold water. Pour it into a sauce pan with the water and salt. Bring the water to a boil, then down to a simmer. Continue cooking until all the water is absorbed.
♦ Sauté the onion in the olive oil until it is lightly browned. Add the garlic, and sauté 1 minute. Add the rice, and toss the mixture. Add the tomato fondue, mustard, parsley, salt, pepper, and pecans. Toss to blend well, and serve.

Pillar House Whipped Potatoes

(TO COOK THE POTATOES)
½ teaspoon salt
1½ pounds peeled all-purpose potatoes

(TO PURÉE THE POTATOES)

2 ounces butter	salt and white pepper
⅓ cup half and half	pinch nutmeg

(TO COOK THE POTATOES)

♦ Boil the potatoes in 2 quarts water with the ½ teaspoon salt until the potatoes are tender, but still firm. Drain them, then place them on a pan in a 200°F oven until they are completely dry.

(TO PURÉE THE POTATOES)

♦ Purée the potatoes with a food mill, mashing tool, or hand-held electric mixer. (*Do not* use a food processor, which would leave you with a sticky mass of soft, glutinous starch.)

- Warm the half and half, then add it to the potatoes along with the butter, salt, and pepper to taste, and the nutmeg. Stir well to blend all. Use a pastry bag to pipe out the potatoes as a border, or serve them as a separate accompaniment.

Garlic Creamed Potatoes

butter
1 pound all-purpose potatoes, peeled and sliced ¼-inch thick
2 cups milk
3 cloves garlic, minced
¼ teaspoon salt

¼ teaspoon white pepper
1 bay leaf
1 cup heavy cream
¼ cup dried bread crumbs
¼ cup fresh-grated parmesan cheese
½ cup swiss cheese, grated

- Preheat an oven to 325°F.
- Lightly butter a casserole dish. Arrange the potato slices in close rows, overlapping the slices within each row.
- Combine the milk, 2 cloves minced garlic, salt, pepper, and bay leaf. Pour the liquid over the potatoes. Cover the dish, and bake 25 minutes, or until the potatoes are al dente. Pour off the excess milk.
- Turn the oven up to 400°F.
- Combine the heavy cream and 1 clove minced garlic, and pour over the potatoes. Sprinkle the parmesan and swiss cheese, then the bread crumbs, over the top. Bake 10 minutes, or until the cheese is golden brown and bubbling.

Roasted Red Potatoes

4 ounces butter
1 medium onion, sliced into very thin rounds
1 shallot, minced
2 cloves garlic, minced
12 medium red-skinned potatoes, scrubbed and quartered

¼ teaspoon salt
¼ teaspoon pepper
1 teaspoon dried rosemary, crushed

- Preheat an oven to 400°F.
- In a heavy ovenproof skillet, melt the butter. Sauté the onion, shallot, and garlic. Add the remaining ingredients, stir, then place the skillet in the oven. Cook 30 minutes, or until the potatoes are done.

Potatoes Pear William

2 large egg yolks
2 tablespoons pear brandy
Pillar House Whipped Potatoes (page 70) *without* the half and half
flour seasoned with salt, white pepper, and paprika

6 eggs, beaten
3 cups seasoned dry bread crumbs (see page 39)
vegetable oil for deep frying
1 bunch parsley

♦ Whip the egg yolks and the pear brandy into the potato mixture.
♦ With your hands slightly moistened with water, carefully mold approximately 4 ounces of the potato mixture into the shape of a pear. Repeat this until all the potato mixture is used. Place the potato pears on a tray or plate in the refrigerator for 30 minutes to chill.
♦ One at a time, dust the potato pears lightly with flour. Dip them into the beaten eggs to coat them, allowing the excess egg to drip off. Then coat them with the bread crumbs. Place them in the refrigerator to set.
♦ Pour the oil into a heavy-gauge pan to a depth of at least 3 inches. Adjust the flame to bring the temperature of the oil to 365°F.
♦ Drop the potato pears into the hot fat, and fry them until they are golden brown. Keep the fried potatoes hot in a 325°F oven until all are ready. Poke a small hole into the top of each potato, and insert a sprig of parsley as garnish.

Potatoes au Gratin

1 pound red-skinned potatoes
½ ounce butter
1 clove garlic, minced
½ cup leeks, well rinsed and diced small

1½ cups half and half
¼ teaspoon salt
¼ teaspoon white pepper
⅛ teaspoon nutmeg
1 cup heavy cream

♦ Peel the potatoes, and slice them crosswise ⅛-inch thick. Immerse the slices in cold water until you are ready to use them.
♦ Preheat an oven to 300°F.
♦ Rub the interior of a casserole dish with the butter. Sprinkle the minced garlic into the dish.
♦ Lay half the potatoes in the dish. Sprinkle the leeks over the potatoes. Sprinkle with half the salt, pepper, and nutmeg. Top with the remaining potato slices, then the remaining salt, pepper, and nutmeg.
♦ Pour the cream over all, cover the dish, and bake 1 hour. Remove the cover, and continue baking 20 minutes, or until the potatoes are tender and browned on top.

6 · Breads

From the garde manger, or pantry department (left to right): Ramona Cook, Michael Johnson, and Tommy Markham.

Pecan Rolls

(DOUGH)

1½ teaspoons salt
½ cup sugar
2 tablespoons (2 packages) dry yeast
1 pound, 11 ounces (about 5½ cups) flour

1 tablespoon cinnamon
1 teaspoon nutmeg
¾ cup milk
3 large eggs
12 ounces butter, melted

(GLAZE)

12 ounces (about 2 cups) brown sugar
6 ounces unsalted butter

4 ounces (about ⅓ cup) honey
¼ cup water

(TO ASSEMBLE)

the glaze
the dough

1 cup chopped pecans

(DOUGH)

♦ Put all the dough ingredients except the milk, eggs, and butter into the bowl of an electric mixer. Blend together, then add the remaining ingredients. Beat the dough with a dough hook until it is smooth and elastic. Wrap it in plastic, and refrigerate it.

(GLAZE)

♦ With a rotary mixer, beat the sugar and butter in a bowl until the mixture is creamy. Add the honey, and blend. Add the water, and blend.

(TO ASSEMBLE)

♦ Lightly butter 4 6-cup muffin tins. Place about 2 tablespoons of the glaze in each cup.
♦ Roll the dough out on a floured board to a rectangle measuring approximately 18 by 28 inches. Sprinkle the pecans over the dough, and press them in with the rolling pin. Beginning at one

of the longer edges, roll the dough into a tight cylinder. Cut the cylinder into approximately 24 1-inch slices, and place each slice in one of the muffin cups. Allow the rolls to rise in a warm place for 45 minutes, or until they are slightly puffed.
- ♦ Preheat an oven to 375°F.
- ♦ Bake the rolls 20 minutes, or until they are golden brown and the sugar has caramelized. Serve them warm. Makes 2 dozen.

Anadama Bread

1 tablespoon (1 package) dry yeast	1 tablespoon salt
1 teaspoon sugar	¾ cup warm water
1¼ cup warm water	½ cup yellow cornmeal
1 ounce butter	3½ cups flour
4 tablespoons molasses	vegetable oil

- ♦ Stir the yeast and sugar into ½ cup warm water until the yeast and sugar are dissolved.
- ♦ Combine the butter, molasses, and salt with ¾ cup warm water, and stir until all are well blended.
- ♦ Combine the two liquid mixtures in a large mixing bowl. Stir in the cornmeal and 1 cup of the flour, and blend well. Add the remaining flour, and stir until the dough comes away from the side of the bowl. Turn out the dough onto a well-floured board. Knead 10 minutes, until the dough is smooth and elastic.
- ♦ Coat the inside of another large bowl with vegetable oil. Place the dough into this bowl, cover it with a clean, damp cloth, and set it in a warm place. Allow the dough to rise approximately 2 hours, or until it is doubled in bulk.
- ♦ Punch the dough down, place it on a lightly floured board, and knead it briefly. Press it into a rectangle, then turn each of the four sides into the center. Pinch the edges together, and turn the dough over. Put it into an oiled baking pan (about 9 by 5 by 3 inches in size). Cover the pan with the damp cloth, set it in a warm place, and allow the dough to rise about 1 hour, or until it is doubled in size.
- ♦ Preheat an oven to 425°F.
- ♦ When the dough has doubled in size the second time, place the pan in the oven. After 10 minutes turn the temperature down to 400°F, and continue baking another 20 minutes. When the top of the loaf is golden brown, and the bread sounds hollow when tapped with the back of metal spoon, remove the pan from the oven. Allow the bread to cool 10 minutes, then remove it from the pan.
- ♦ If you don't serve the bread immediately, store it in a plastic bag until you are ready to slice it. Toasted and buttered, it makes an excellent breakfast.

To activate yeast, the temperature of the water should be about 100°F. If the water is too hot, it will destroy the yeast. If it is not warm enough, the yeast may not develop properly. You may wish to check the water temperature with a pastry thermometer until you develop a feel for it.

Different crops of wheat can produce flours with different moisture contents. Therefore, the quantity of flour required for a recipe may have to be adjusted. During the mixing, use enough flour that the dough comes away from the sides of the bowl when you stir it. During the initial kneading, toss flour onto the board until the dough no longer sticks to it.

Kneading is an important step in baking bread. This physical pushing and pulling develops the gluten, a naturally occurring element in flour that gives the bread its elasticity and chewiness.

For its first rising, you might put the dough into a gas oven with only the pilot light on. With the oven door closed, the pilot light will emit enough heat to allow the yeast to multiply, and thus the dough to rise. The temperature recommended for this step is 95°F.

Gingered Biscuits

1⅓ cup flour
1½ tablespoons cornstarch
¾ tablespoon orange zest
  (from 1 large orange)
¾ tablespoon lemon zest (from
  2 lemons)
1 teaspoon ginger
⅛ teaspoon salt

1½ teaspoons baking powder
⅛ teaspoon baking soda
3 ounces unsalted butter
½ cup half and half
2¼ teaspoons lemon juice
1 egg, beaten
sugar

- ◆ Combine all the dry ingredients (the first 8) in a large mixing bowl, and stir until blended.
- ◆ Add the butter, the half and half, and the lemon juice. Stir just until the ingredients are blended; do not overwork the dough.
- ◆ Preheat an oven to 400°F.
- ◆ Turn the dough out onto a floured board, and roll it into a rectangle about ¼-inch thick. Using a 3-inch round, fluted biscuit cutter, cut out the biscuits, and place them on a buttered baking sheet. Brush each biscuit with the egg wash, then sprinkle lightly with sugar.
- ◆ Bake 15 minutes, or until the biscuits are golden brown.

Dill and Onion Rolls

(DOUGH)
1 large egg
1 cup cottage cheese
4 tablespoons sugar
¼ cup onions, minced
¾ ounces butter, melted
4 teaspoons dill seed

2½ teaspoons salt
¼ teaspoon baking soda
¼ cup warm water
1 tablespoon (1 package) dry
  yeast
3¾ cups flour

(TO BAKE)
the dough
vegetable oil
yellow cornmeal

1 ounce butter, melted
salt

(DOUGH)
- ◆ In a large mixing bowl, combine the first 8 ingredients. Blend well with a wooden spoon.
- ◆ In another bowl combine the yeast and warm water. Stir to blend well. Combine the two mixtures.
- ◆ Add the flour, and mix until the dough comes away from the sides of the bowl. Turn the dough onto a floured board, and knead for 10 minutes, or until the dough is smooth and elastic.
- ◆ Place the dough in another large bowl lightly coated with vegetable oil. Cover the bowl with a damp, clean cloth, put it in a

Biscuit dough, like pie and cookie dough, is referred to as a short dough. A short dough is rich in fat. The fat is called shortening because it shortens the gluten strands in the flour. Whereas you knead a yeast dough to develop the gluten and thus make the bread chewy and elastic, you must avoid overworking a short dough. Biscuits, pie crusts, shortbreads, and most cookies are intended to be light and flaky. It is minimal handling of the dough, as well as the presence of shortening, that makes them this way.

A fluted biscuit cutter is a circular metal form with a squiggly edge. If you don't have this utensil, you can use an unfluted biscuit cutter or even an inverted cup or glass.

After cutting all the biscuits you can from the first sheet of dough, press the scraps together, roll out the remaining dough ¼-inch thick, and cut out more biscuits. As before, avoid overworking the dough.

warm place, and allow the dough to rise until it is doubled in size (about 1½ hours).

(TO BAKE)
- Preheat an oven to 375°F.
- Punch the dough down, and turn it out onto the floured board. Divide the dough into 18 equal pieces. Roll each piece with the palm of your hand until it is nicely rounded. Grease 2 cookie sheets with vegetable oil, and sprinkle them lightly with yellow cornmeal. Place the dough balls on the baking sheets, three inches apart. Set the baking sheets in a warm place for about 45 minutes, or until the rolls are doubled in size.
- Bake the rolls 17 to 20 minutes, or until they are golden brown. Remove them from the oven, brush them with melted butter, and sprinkle them lightly with salt. Serve hot.

7 · *Final Courses*

Douglas Catania and David Hernandez, pastry virtuosos.

CHOCOLATE

Reine de Saba

(GANACHE)
1½ pounds semisweet
  chocolate

3 cups heavy cream
4 ounces unsalted butter

(BATTER)
11 ounces semisweet chocolate
11 ounces unsalted butter,
  softened
9 ounces (about 1¼ cups)
  sugar

2 ounces (about ½ cup) flour
10 large eggs
11 ounces (about 2½ cups)
  ground raw almonds

(GARNISH)
the *ganache*
½ cup ground toasted almonds

16 candied violets
2 ounces semisweet chocolate

A food processor is the best tool for grinding almonds.

Candied violets are not truly flowers turned into candy. Rather, they are a lavender-colored sugar confection in the shape of violet petals. If they are not available in a local confectionery or gourmet shop, substitute any small candy that would embellish this rich cake.

To cut the cake more easily, dip the knife into hot water before each slice.

(GANACHE)
♦ Put the chocolate, cream, and butter into the top section of a double boiler. Over a medium flame, heat and stir until the butter and chocolate are completely melted and the ingredients are well blended. Allow the mixture to cool, then refrigerate it.

(BATTER)
♦ Melt the chocolate in a double boiler. Allow it to cool slightly.
♦ In a mixer, beat the 11 ounces butter with the sugar until the mixture is light and creamy. Add the flour and the chocolate, and blend well. Add the eggs one at a time, incorporating each one before adding the next. Add the ground almonds, and blend well.
♦ Preheat an oven to 350°F.
♦ Cut out a 9-inch circle of parchment or wax paper. Butter the inside bottom of a 9-inch cake pan. Lay the paper circle in the

pan, then butter the sides of the pan and the top of the paper. Transfer the cake batter to the pan. Bake 1 hour, or until the cake is firm but still moist at the center.

♦ Allow the cake to cool 10 minutes in the pan. Then turn it out onto a 9-inch round corrugated cardboard circle, and allow it to cool to room temperature.

(GARNISH)

♦ Take the *ganache* out of the refrigerator, and allow it to soften at room temperature. When it is soft, use a cake spatula to spread a thin layer of *ganache* over the top and sides of the cake. Gently press the crushed almonds over the sides of the cake. Spoon the remaining *ganache* into a pastry bag with a #7 star tip. Pipe out 16 rosettes around the top edge of the cake. (For tips on using a pastry bag, see page 16.) Press a candied violet into the center of each rosette.

♦ Melt the remaining 2 ounces chocolate in a double boiler. Transfer the chocolate to a small pastry bag fitted with a #2 round tip (a very small opening). Pipe out a rough lattice—two sets of lines crossing at a 90-degree angle—on the top of the cake. Chill the cake at least 1 hour in the refrigerator.

Wine recommendation: 1984 Robert Mondavi Moscato d'Oro (California), 1986 Essensia Orange Muscat (California), or Dow's Ruby Port (Portugal)

Cappuccino Torte

(CAKE)

2 tablespoons flour	6 egg whites
pinch cinnamon	¾ cup sugar
7 ounces (about 1½ cups) ground toasted almonds	

(GANACHE)

6 ounces (about 1 cup) semisweet chocolate	½ tablespoon dark rum
¾ cup heavy cream	1 ounce butter

(CARAMEL-ALMOND FILLING)

1¾ ounces (about 3 tablespoons) almond paste (marzipan)	1½ tablespoons sugar
1½ tablespoons water	3 tablespoons unsalted butter, softened

(CINNAMON FILLING)

2½ tablespoons unsalted butter, softened	¾ teaspoon cinnamon

(SWISS MERINGUE)
2 small egg whites
pinch salt
¼ cup sugar

⅔ cup heavy cream
¾ tablespoon confectionary
   sugar

(TO ASSEMBLE)
the *ganache*
the cake rectangles
the cinnamon filling

the caramel-almond filling
confectionary sugar
cocoa powder

(CAKE)
- Butter an 11-by-17-inch sheet pan, and dust it lightly with flour. Preheat an oven to 350°F.
- Combine the flour, cinnamon, and ground almonds.
- In another bowl, beat the egg whites to soft peaks. While still beating, slowly add the sugar. Beat until all the sugar is incorporated and the whites form stiff peaks. Fold in the dry ingredients, one-third at a time. Spread the batter evenly in the sheet pan. Bake the cake 8 to 10 minutes, until its edges come away from the sides of the pan and its center is firm. Allow the cake to cool, then turn it out onto a work surface. Trim its edges square, then cut it across the width into 4 equal rectangles. Set these aside.

(GANACHE)
- Put all ingredients into the top of a double boiler. Heat and stir until the chocolate and butter are melted and the mixture is fully blended. Chill in the refrigerator.

(CARAMEL-ALMOND FILLING)
- With a wooden spoon, blend the almond paste with 1 tablespoon water in a small bowl.
- In a small pan over high heat, cook the sugar and ½ tablespoon water to a light caramel (this takes about 1 minute). Pour the caramel into the softened almond paste, and blend it in.
- Beat the softened butter until it is light and creamy, then blend it with the almond-caramel mixture. Set the filling aside.

(CINNAMON FILLING)
- Beat the softened butter with the cinnamon.

(SWISS MERINGUE)
- Beat the whites with the salt to soft peaks. Add the sugar slowly, and continue beating to stiff peaks. Fold half of this mixture into the cinnamon filling. Fold the other half into the caramel-almond filling.
- Whip the cream with the confectionary sugar. Fold half the whipped cream into the cinnamon filling and half into the caramel filling.

(TO ASSEMBLE)

♦ Spread the *ganache* over one of the cake rectangles. Place a second cake rectangle over this. Spread the cinnamon filling on top of the second cake rectangle. Top with a third rectangle. Spread the caramel-almond filling on this layer. Top with the last layer of cake. Dust the top with confectionary sugar, then cocoa. Chill the cake in the refrigerator at least 1 hour before serving.

White Chocolate Pie

Chocolate curls are made by holding a knife blade vertically across a chunk of chocolate, then dragging the knife across the chocolate. Since this requires a fairly large piece of chocolate, you may wish to simply grate a small amount of sweet chocolate, and sprinkle this on top.

(CRUST)

2¼ ounces semisweet chocolate	1½ cups graham cracker crumbs
3 ounces unsalted butter	2¼ tablespoons sugar

(FILLING)

1 tablespoon unflavored granulated gelatin	2 large eggs, separated
⅓ cup white crème de cacao	⅓ cup plus 1 tablespoon sugar
2 ounces white chocolate	1 cup milk
	¾ cup heavy cream, whipped

(GARNISH)

1 cup heavy cream	1 ounce semisweet chocolate, grated
1 tablespoon confectionary sugar	chocolate curls
dash vanilla extract	

♦ Preheat an oven to 300°F.

(CRUST)

♦ Melt the chocolate and butter in a double boiler. Combine the cracker crumbs and sugar. Stir all together until blended, then press the mixture into a buttered 10-inch pie tin. Bake 10 minutes. Set the tin aside, and allow the crust to cool.

(FILLING)

♦ Dissolve the gelatin in the liqueur, and set aside.
♦ Melt the white chocolate in a double boiler. Allow it to cool.
♦ Whip the yolks with ⅓ cup sugar until the mixture is light and slightly thickened.
♦ In a sauce pan, scald the milk. While stirring constantly, pour the milk slowly into the yolks. Return the mixture to the sauce pan, and, while stirring, heat it over a medium flame until it is smooth and thickened. Remove the pan from the fire, and stir in the gelatin-liqueur blend.
♦ Add the melted white chocolate, and stir to blend well. Place the pan in a bowl of ice, and stir until the mixture begins to set. Remove from ice.

- Beat the egg whites with 1 tablespoon sugar to a stiff peak.
- Fold the egg whites and the whipped cream into the chilled chocolate mixture.
- Pour the filling into the prebaked pie shell, smooth the top with a spatula, then chill 1 hour to set the filling.

(GARNISH)
- Whip the cream with the confectionary sugar and vanilla extract.
- Fold the grated chocolate into the whipped cream, and spread the cream over the top of the pie. Top with the chocolate curls.

Bittersweet Chocolate and Grand Marnier Mousse

(CANDIED ORANGE SLICES)
2¼-inch thick round slices of orange, halved and seeded
½ cup water

3 tablespoons sugar
1 teaspoon vanilla extract

(MOUSSE)
2 ounces bittersweet chocolate
1 egg, separated
2 tablespoons water

3 tablespoons Grand Marnier
½ cup heavy cream, whipped
1 tablespoon sugar

(GARNISH)
¼ cup toasted almonds
½ cup heavy cream, whipped

the candied orange slices

(CANDIED ORANGE SLICES)
- Combine the water, sugar, and vanilla in a sauce pan. Bring to a boil, and simmer 5 minutes. Add the four orange pieces, and simmer 15 minutes. Remove the pan from the fire, and set it aside, leaving the orange slices sitting in the syrup.

(MOUSSE)
- Melt the chocolate in a double boiler. When the chocolate is fully melted, remove the bowl and set it aside. Allow the chocolate to cool slightly.
- Combine the egg yolk, water, and Grand Marnier in the top of a double boiler over barely simmering water. Whip the mixture until it is thick and roughly doubled in volume. Remove the bowl from the fire, and gently stir in the chocolate. Set aside.
- Whip the cream until it forms stiff peaks. Place it in the refrigerator.
- While slowly adding the sugar, whip the egg white until it forms stiff peaks.
- Gently fold the whipped cream into the chocolate mixture. When it is almost completely blended, *very gently* fold in the whipped

Make your own vanilla sugar by putting granulated sugar into a container along with a vanilla bean or two. Over a period of weeks, the aroma and flavor of the vanilla bean will permeate the sugar. Use the vanilla-flavored sugar, and omit the vanilla extract, in recipes calling for both extract and granulated sugar. As you remove vanilla sugar from the container, replace it with more granulated sugar.

When whipping egg whites, it is essential that the bowl you use is free of any trace of fat or oil. Otherwise the whites won't whip. To counter any possible presence of fat or oil, which is alkaline, some cooks add an acid, such as salt, lemon juice, or cream of tartar.

Be careful when whipping heavy cream. If it is overwhipped it will turn into butter. If this should happen, simply pour off the liquid in the bowl, wrap the butter in cheesecloth, and gently massage the mass until all the remaining liquid has dripped out. Use as any other unsalted butter.

egg white. Continue folding until all the ingredients are fully blended. Place the bowl in the refrigerator, cover it, and allow the mousse to chill 30 minutes.

◆ Fill a pastry bag fitted with a #9 star tip with the mousse mixture. Using a swirling motion, fill 4 champagne saucers, large wine goblets, or other appropriate dishes with the mousse.

(GARNISH)

◆ Decorate each dish with a whipped cream rosette, a sprinkle of toasted almonds, and a piece of candied orange.

Chocolate Pâté, Pistachio Sauce

(PRALINE)

¼ cup sliced almonds | ¼ cup sugar

(PÂTÉ)

7 tablespoons plus 5 tablespoons heavy cream
½ pound bittersweet chocolate
2 ounces unsalted butter

2 tablespoons ground praline
1½ tablespoons Grand Marnier
5 ounces white chocolate

(PISTACHIO SAUCE)

3 egg yolks
⅓ cup sugar
1 cup milk

½ cup shelled unsalted pistachios, roughly chopped

(PRALINE)

◆ Cook the sugar and almonds in a small sauté or sauce pan until they are lightly caramelized. Pour the praline onto a greased pan or onto greased parchment paper. Allow it to cool and harden. Break it up into small pieces, then put it into a food processor and pulverize it.

(PÂTÉ)

◆ In a double boiler, heat the 7 tablespoons cream, and melt the chocolate and butter in it. Divide the hot mixture into two equal portions. Stir the praline into one, the Grand Marnier into the other.

◆ Cut out a rectangle of parchment or wax paper to fit into the bottom of a loaf pan. Lightly butter the bottom of the pan, then lay in the cut paper. Lightly butter the top of the paper and the sides of the pan.

◆ Pour the Grand Marnier-chocolate mixture into the loaf pan. Refrigerate until it has set.

◆ In a double boiler, melt the white chocolate in the remaining 5 tablespoons cream. Allow the mixture to cool to room temperature.

- Pour the white chocolate mixture onto the chilled Grand Marnier layer. Refrigerate until the new layer has set.
- Pour the praline-chocolate mixture onto the white chocolate layer. Refrigerate until the third layer has set.

(PISTACHIO SAUCE)
- Beat the egg yolks and sugar in a small bowl until the mixture is light and slightly thickened.
- In a sauce pan, scald the milk. While constantly stirring, pour it slowly into the yolk mixture. Pour the milk-yolk-sugar mixture into the sauce pan. Heat, while stirring, until the mixture is smooth and thickened. Add the chopped pistachios, and allow the sauce to cool.
- To remove the pâté, dip the mold into very hot water for 5 seconds, then invert it onto a serving platter. Use a knife dipped into hot water to slice the pâté. Pour the Pistachio Sauce over each slice.

FRUIT

Praline and Peach Cheesecake

(CRUST)
¾ cup graham cracker crumbs ¼ cup ground hazelnuts
¼ cup sugar 2½ ounces butter, melted

(CHEESECAKE)
2 pounds cream cheese ½ cup heavy cream
1 cup sugar 6 peach halves, cut into 6
7 eggs wedges each

(PRALINE)
1 cup sliced almonds ¾ cup sugar

(ICING AND GARNISH)
2 cups heavy cream 3 peach halves, cut into 6
¼ teaspoon vanilla extract wedges each
the ground praline

(CRUST)
- Combine the cracker crumbs, sugar, hazelnuts, and butter in a small bowl, and stir to blend well. Press this mixture into the bottom of a 10-inch springform pan. Set the pan aside.
- Preheat an oven to 225°F.

(CHEESECAKE)

♦ Beat the cheese with an electric mixer until it is soft and smooth. While mixing, add the sugar slowly. Continue mixing, scraping the sides of the bowl occasionally, until the sugar is well blended. Add the eggs one at a time, incorporating each before adding the next. Add the heavy cream, and beat it in.

♦ Arrange the 36 peach wedges in concentric circles on top of the pie crust. Pour the cheesecake batter over the peaches, and tap the springform pan onto the counter several times to settle the batter. Place the pan on a baking sheet, and bake the cheesecake 2½ hours. Allow it to cool completely, then remove the outer band of the springform pan. Place the cheesecake in the refrigerator.

(PRALINE)

♦ Place the almonds and sugar in a small pan over a medium flame, and cook until the sugar caramelizes to light brown. Remove the pan from the fire, and pour the praline onto a pan that is either lightly oiled or covered with a sheet of wax or parchment paper. Allow the praline to cool completely, until it is hard and brittle. Remove it from the pan or paper, break it into small pieces, and pulverize it in a food processor.

(ICING AND GARNISH)

♦ Whip 1¼ cups of the heavy cream with the vanilla, gradually sprinkling in ⅓ cup of the pulverized praline. Ice the cheesecake with the whipped cream, smoothing the top and sides with an icing spatula.

♦ Lift the cheesecake, and rest it on the palm of one hand. Over a clean pan, gently press some of the ground praline around the side of the cheesecake.

♦ Take a 9-inch-square piece of poster board, and cut out a 3-inch circle in the center. Lay this template gently over the center of the cheesecake. Sprinkle the remaining praline mixture over the circle. Remove the template.

♦ Whip the remaining ¾ cup of heavy cream. Fill a pastry bag fitted with a #7 star tip. Pipe out 16 rosettes around the top edge of the cheesecake. Between each rosette and the circle of praline, place a wedge of peach.

♦ Refrigerate the cheesecake until it is well chilled (at least 2 hours).

Wine recommendation: Nashoba Valley Peach (Massachusetts)

Raspberry Charlotte Royale

(RASPBERRY SAUCE)
1 8-ounce package frozen
   raspberries in syrup

sugar
raspberry brandy (optional)

(CAKES)
2 cups sliced almonds
1¼ cups plus 5 tablespoons
   sugar
6 large eggs
½ cup flour

whites of 6 large eggs
pinch salt
3 tablespoons melted butter,
   cooled

(TO ASSEMBLE)
the cakes
raspberry preserves
Raspberry Bavarian Cream
   (page 92)

Raspberry Sauce

(RASPBERRY SAUCE)
♦ Purée the thawed raspberries in a food processor. Sweeten them
   with sugar if necessary. Add raspberry brandy if desired. Press
   the raspberries through a fine sieve, and set them aside.

(CAKES)
♦ Pulverize the almonds with the sugar in a food processor. Set
   the mixture aside.
♦ In a small bowl, beat the 6 eggs with a rotary mixer. While
   beating, slowly add 1¼ cups sugar. Beat a total of about 8
   minutes, or until the egg-sugar mixture is light and creamy. Add
   the pulverized almonds, and continue mixing 1 minute. Sift the
   flour into this mixture, and blend.
♦ Preheat an oven to 400°F. Grease and lightly flour two 11-by-
   17-inch sheet pans.
♦ Beat the egg whites with the salt to soft peaks. Add the 5 tablespoons sugar while beating. Continue beating until the whites
   form stiff peaks.
♦ Fold half the meringue into the yolk mixture. Fold in the second
   half. Add the melted butter, and stir to blend all.
♦ Divide the batter between the two pans, spreading it evenly with
   a spatula. Bake 8 to 10 minutes, or until the cakes are golden
   brown and spring back when touched. Let them cool in the pans
   10 minutes, then invert them onto separate large sheets of parchment paper. Allow them to cool to room temperature, about 30
   minutes.

(TO ASSEMBLE)
♦ Spread both cakes with a layer of raspberry preserves. Roll each
   sponge into a tight roll, using the parchment paper and a yard-

stick to assist. (After the first two turns, press the edge of the parchment paper into the fold of the roll. Press the yardstick firmly against the parchment paper, tightening the roll. Remove the parchment paper, and make another two or three turns of the roll. With a damp sponge, wipe off any raspberry preserves that may have adhered to the parchment paper, and press the paper and the yardstick into the fold of the roll. Repeat this procedure once more to ensure a tight, firm roll. Wrap the rolls in the parchment paper, and put them into the refrigerator to set.

♦ Line a charlotte mold or stainless steel bowl with plastic wrap so the plastic wrap extends over the edge of the mold. Slice one of the rolls into ⅜-inch-thick spiral rounds. Lay these rounds in the plastic wrap–lined mold, pressing and shaping them so they completely cover the interior surface. If any of the rounds extend out of the mold, trim them flush with the edge.

♦ Fill the mold with Raspberry Bavarian Cream to ½ inch below the edge. Slice the second roll as you did the first. Cover the Raspberry Bavarian Cream with the spiral rounds, pressed together to completely seal the dish. Cover the charlotte, and allow it to chill in the refrigerator 4 hours.

♦ Invert the charlotte onto a serving platter, carefully remove the mold, and lift off the plastic wrap. Serve the Raspberry Sauce separately.

Raspberries au Gratin

3 large egg yolks	½ teaspoon vanilla extract
⅓ cup sugar	1½ pints raspberries
½ cup milk	brown sugar
½ cup heavy cream	2 sprigs mint

♦ Whip the yolks and sugar until the mixture is light and slightly thickened.

♦ Combine the milk, cream, and vanilla in a sauce pan, and heat to scalding. While stirring constantly, slowly pour the milk and cream into the beaten yolks and sugar. Return this mixture to the fire, stirring constantly while heating. When the sauce is thick and creamy, remove it from the fire.

♦ Preheat a broiler.

♦ Divide the sauce among four ovenproof casserole dishes. Fill the dishes with equal portions of raspberries, and sprinkle brown sugar over.

♦ Under a broiler, brown the tops of the casseroles. Garnish with mint.

Wine recommendation: Banfi Asti Spumanti (Italy)

Strawberry Millefeuille with Strawberry Sauce

(PUFF PASTRY DOUGH)

1 pound unsalted butter, softened

1 pound (3 cups plus 2 tablespoons) flour

1 cup cold water

½ teaspoon salt

(PASTRY CREAM)

3 tablespoons flour

3 tablespoons cornstarch

¾ cup sugar

4 egg yolks

2 cups milk

¼ teaspoon vanilla extract

(TO ASSEMBLE)

the puff pastry dough

the pastry cream

2 pints ripe strawberries, gently rinsed, their tops removed, and sliced ¼-inch thick

(STRAWBERRY SAUCE)

2 4-ounce packages frozen strawberries

1 tablespoon confectionary sugar, sifted

3 tablespoons kirschwasser

(GARNISH)

confectionary sugar

1 bunch mint

the strawberry sauce

(PUFF PASTRY DOUGH)

- Place the butter in a bowl with ⅓ cup of the flour. Blend with a rotary mixer until smooth.
- Place the butter-flour mixture on a lightly floured board, and shape it into a square approximately 1-inch thick. Refrigerate it.
- Put the remaining flour and salt in a mixing bowl with the cold water. Mix until the dough is fully blended and comes away from the sides of the bowl. (Add a little more flour if the dough is too wet to pull away from the sides.)
- Knead this dough on a floured board about 5 minutes, until it is smooth and elastic. Roll it into a sphere. Cut an X three-quarters of the way down into the ball. Press each section outward, dust with flour, and roll out the dough in the shape of a four-leaf clover.
- Place the square cake of butter in the center of the dough. Fold each of the four leaves over the butter, totally encasing it. Roll

The most important procedure in making puff pastry dough is ensuring all corners are square at all times. Also, be sure a corner folded over another corner sits squarely in alignment.

The French word millefeuille (a thousand leaves) aptly describes the unique nature of puff pastry dough. Without a leavening agent, such as yeast, baking powder, or baking soda, it rises into a multilayered, light and flaky, exceptionally palatable, and crisp pastry. The rising takes place by virtue of literally thousands of layers of flour and butter. The initial dough, of cloverleaf shape folded over a block of butter, results in three layers: dough, butter, dough. When this is rolled out, then folded into thirds, you have nine layers of butter and flour. With the three-fold process repeated five additional times, the final result is 2,187 layers of butter and flour. When heat is applied to this dough, the butter melts and the water in the butter boils, producing steam. This steam expands and pushes up the minute layers of flour.

The historical origin of puff pastry dough (feuilletage) is thoroughly disputed. Some say it was invented in ancient Greece, whose literature includes mention of a flaky pastry. Although Greece is known for a family of flaky pastries (baklava and spanakopita being two well-known varieties), they are not produced by kinetic reaction, the result of the repeated folding into thousands of layers. Rather, they are created by layering a paper-thin dough (phyllo, or filo, with which we make Apple Strudel, pages 93–94) and brushing each layer with melted butter. This technique does indeed produce a flaky pastry, but not by virtue of a dough that itself comprises thousands of layers.

As far as we know, French is the only cuisine that has traditionally produced this dough. Depending which historian you believe, its creator is either Claude Gelée, a celebrated seventeenth-century painter from Lorraine, or a chef from the aristocratic house of Condé by the name of Feuillet. Since feuilletage *likely takes its name from its nature, not its creator, we suspect Gelée deserves the credit.*

Puff pastry dough is also available ready-made. Pepperidge Farms makes a reasonably good variety, in both sheets and pre-cut rounds. For this recipe you'll need 1 pound commercial dough, in sheet form.

the dough into a large rectangle, remove it to a sheet pan, and refrigerate it for 15 minutes.

- ◆ Return the dough rectangle to a floured board, and roll it out into a slightly larger rectangle, making sure all corners are square. With a dry pastry brush, brush off all traces of flour from the top surface. With the longer sides of the rectangle running left to right in front of you, lift the upper and lower right-hand corners, and fold over a third of the dough. Brush off excess flour. Lift the upper and lower left-hand corners, and fold this end over the rest of the dough. Turn the dough 90 degrees, and roll it out into another rectangle. Place it back on the sheet pan, pressing a finger into one edge of the dough, and return it to the refrigerator for another 15 minutes.
- ◆ Repeat this process of rolling out, folding in thirds, and chilling 5 more times, marking each turn by making small indentations with your finger.
- ◆ When you are finished, cut the dough into two equal portions. Wrap it air-tight, and freeze or refrigerate it until you are ready to use it. Puff pastry dough will last 2 weeks in the refrigerator and up to 6 months in the freezer.

(PASTRY CREAM)
- ◆ Combine the flour, cornstarch, sugar, egg yolks, and ½ cup milk in a mixing bowl, and blend together.
- ◆ Heat 1½ cups milk with the vanilla, and bring to a boil. Remove the hot milk from the fire immediately.
- ◆ Using a ladle, *very slowly* pour the hot milk into the flour, cornstarch, sugar, yolk, and milk mixture, whipping constantly. When all the milk has been incorporated, pour the pastry cream into the pan in which you heated the milk. Stir constantly, with a wooden spoon, as the pastry cream slowly cooks and thickens. Continue stirring until it begins to simmer, then stir, as it simmers 3 minutes more. Remove the pan from the fire, and transfer the pastry cream to a stainless steel or glass bowl that is still wet from a rinsing with cold water. Cover the pastry cream with paper butter wrappers. Allow it to cool, then refrigerate it.

(TO ASSEMBLE)
- ◆ Preheat an oven to 400°F.
- ◆ On a lightly floured board, roll out the puff pastry into a rectangle 11 inches by 16 inches by ¼-inch thick. Remove it to a baking sheet, lightly buttered or covered with a sheet of parchment paper. Tap a fork gently over the surface of this dough, making small punctures all over it. Place the baking sheet in the oven, and bake 30 to 35 minutes, or until the pastry is golden brown. (Check the dough once or twice during its baking. If any part of it rises above the rest, puncture the hill with a long fork, and press it down.) Allow the pastry to cool to room temperature.
- ◆ With a serrated knife, trim the pastry so the edges are straight

and the corners are perfect right angles. Cut this pastry "board" lengthwise into three long strips, each approximately 3½ inches wide. Spread a layer of pastry cream, about ⅛-inch thick, over two of the pastry strips. Cover the pastry cream with a layer of the sliced fresh strawberries, set as close together as possible.

♦ Place one of the cream- and fruit-covered strips on top of the other. Place the third strip upside down on top of the stack. Put the pastry into the refrigerator for 30 minutes.

(STRAWBERRY SAUCE)
♦ Purée the frozen strawberries in a food processor along with the sugar and kirschwasser. Press the strawberries through a fine sieve, and set the purée aside.

(GARNISH)
♦ Place the pastry on a cutting board. Very gently slice it across its width, every 2 inches, to make 8 individual pastries. Dust the top of each with confectionary sugar. Garnish with a sprig of fresh mint and some of the sauce, and serve.

Wine recommendation: 1983 Neisteiner Rebach Sylvaner Beeranauslese (Germany)

Poached Pears, Almond Cream

(MOUSSE)
2 ounces semisweet chocolate	½ teaspoon vanilla extract
½ ounce butter	1½ teaspoons sugar
½ cup heavy cream	1 large egg yolk

(SAUCE)
1 cup milk	3 large egg yolks
½ cup sliced almonds	⅓ cup sugar

(PEARS)
juice of 1 lemon	2 cups water
2 large, firm Bartlett (or other variety) pears	½ cup sugar

(GARNISH)
4 ounces puff pastry dough (pages 87–88)	sugar
1 egg, beaten	½ cup sliced almonds

(TO ASSEMBLE)
the cooked pears	the pastry leaves
the sauce	the toasted almonds
the mousse	

The importance of stirring the pastry cream constantly during cooking cannot be overstated. Since this mixture is so thick, it burns very easily. If it scorches on the bottom, the entire mixture will smell and taste burnt. It helps to use a heavy-bottomed sauce pan, which evenly distributes the heat.

The bowl rinsed in cold water helps cool the pastry cream. The film of butter that covers the interior surface of butter wrappers prevents the top of the cream from drying out.

To avoid mashing, shifting, or otherwise destroying this delicate pastry, you must cut it with a serrated knife, or bread knife. A serrated knife is made specifically to cut bread, rolls, cake, and pastry, and to maintain its extremely sharp cutting edge without ever being sharpened.

Kirschwasser ("cherry water") is actually a clear cherry-flavored brandy with a very high alcohol content.

(MOUSSE)
- Place the semisweet chocolate and the butter in a double boiler over simmering water. Heat until the chocolate and butter are melted. Stir to blend. Remove the bowl from the heat, and set it aside.
- Whip the cream with the vanilla, adding the sugar while beating. Continue beating until the cream holds a stiff peak. Set it aside.
- Briskly whip the egg yolk into the melted chocolate and butter. Fold the whipped cream into the chocolate, one-half at a time. When the mixture is smooth and fully blended, cover it, and place it in the refrigerator.

(SAUCE)
- Put the milk into a sauce pan with the almonds. Bring to a boil. Remove the pan from the fire, and let it sit, covered, for 30 minutes.
- In a small stainless steel or glass bowl, beat the eggs and sugar until the sugar is completely dissolved.
- Strain the almonds from the milk, and discard the almonds. Bring the milk to a boil again, and remove it from the fire. With a ladle, *very slowly* pour the milk into the yolk and sugar mixture, and whip vigorously until the milk is fully incorporated. Return this mixture to the pan in which the milk was heated. While constantly stirring, cook the sauce until it comes to a simmer and is slightly thickened. Remove it from the fire, transfer it to a clean container, and allow it to cool. Cover the container, and place it in the refrigerator.

(PEARS)
- Fill a bowl with the lemon juice and enough cold water to cover the pears. Peel the pears with a vegetable peeler, and remove their stems. Remove a ¼-inch slice from the bottom of each pear. Place the pears in the lemon water.
- Bring the 2 cups water and the ½ cup of sugar to a boil in a sauce pan. Place the pears in the syrup, and simmer 20 to 25 minutes, or until the pears are tender but still firm (check by piercing them with a toothpick). *Do not overcook.* Remove the pan from the fire, and allow the pears to cool in the poaching syrup.

(GARNISH)
- Preheat an oven to 375°F.
- Roll out the puff pastry into a rectangle approximately 3 inches by 4 inches by ¼-inch thick. With a paring knife, cut out the shapes of four pear leaves, marking each leaf with a center vein and ancillary veins. Brush them with the egg wash, sprinkle them with sugar, and bake them 15 to 20 minutes, until they are golden brown.
- Place the almonds in a small baking pan, and toast them until

they are golden brown. Be sure to check them, and stir them, every five minutes or so—they burn very easily.

(TO ASSEMBLE)
♦ Remove the pears from the syrup. Cut them in half lengthwise. Using a parisienne scoop, remove their cores. Place the four halves cut side down on a cutting surface, and make eight parallel, lengthwise cuts, about ¼ inch apart, through each half, from the base to one inch from the stem end.
♦ Pour some of the sauce onto each of four plates. Place a sliced pear half on top of the sauce. Gently press down and to one side so the pear half fans out.
♦ Place a scoop of chocolate mousse (or a small rosette piped from a pastry bag; see page 16) on top of each pear, and stick one of the pastry leaves into the mousse. Sprinkle the toasted almonds over the sauce around the pear, and serve.

Mixed Fruit Tart

(PASTRY FOR 2 TART SHELLS)
3 cups flour
10 ounces unsalted butter, cut
   into ½-inch cubes
½ cup sugar

¼ teaspoon salt
1 large egg
yolk of 1 large egg

(LEMON PASTRY CREAM)
yolks of 5 large eggs
3 tablespoons sugar
4½ tablespoons cornstarch
1½ cups milk

¾ teaspoon vanilla extract
zest of 1 lemon
juice of 2 lemons

(TO ASSEMBLE)
the pastry
Lemon Pastry Cream
five varieties of fruit, such as
   oranges, bananas,
   raspberries, strawberries,
   blackberries, blueberries,
   kiwi, pineapple, peaches,
   mangoes, or melon

apricot jelly

(PASTRY)
♦ Combine all ingredients except the egg and the yolk in a large mixing bowl. Mash all together with your hands, until the butter is broken up and distributed throughout. Add the eggs, and blend into a homogenous dough. Divide the dough into 2 equal pieces. Wrap both in plastic. Place one piece in the freezer for future use; place the other in the refrigerator for 20 minutes.

(PASTRY CREAM)

♦ Whip the yolks and the sugar until light and slightly thickened. Sift the cornstarch into the whipped egg yolks, and blend. Combine the milk and the vanilla in a sauce pan, and heat to scalding. While constantly whipping, slowly pour the hot milk into the egg yolks. Return the mixture to the fire, and, while stirring constantly, cook it until it is smooth and thickened. Add the lemon zest and juice, and blend thoroughly. Transfer the pastry cream to a clean bowl, and cover it with a paper wrapper from a stick of butter. Set it aside to cool.

(TO ASSEMBLE)

♦ Preheat an oven to 375°F.
♦ Roll the dough out on a floured board. Press it into a lightly greased tart pan with a removable bottom. Trim the edges of the dough, then "dock" it by piercing it all over with the tines of a fork. Bake the pastry 20 to 25 minutes, or until it is golden brown. Remove it from the oven, and allow it to cool completely.
♦ Remove the rim of the tart form. Stir the chilled pastry cream, and spread a layer of it in the tart shell. Slice your choice of fruit, and arrange it in concentric circles around the tart. Melt the apricot jelly in a small saucepan, and brush it over the top of the tart. Refrigerate the tart at least 1 hour before serving.

Raspberry Bavarian Cream

(SAUCE)

1 8-ounce package frozen raspberries in syrup, thawed	sugar

(BAVARIAN CREAM)

2½ 8-ounce packages (1¼ pounds) frozen raspberries in syrup, thawed	yolks of 5 large eggs
	⅓ cup sugar
	1½ cups milk
1¼ tablespoons unflavored granulated gelatin	1 teaspoon vanilla extract
	1 cup heavy cream, whipped

(GARNISH)

fresh mint	fresh raspberries

(SAUCE)

♦ Purée the single package of raspberries in a food processor. Sweeten with sugar if needed. Press the purée through a fine sieve, and set it aside.

(BAVARIAN CREAM)

♦ Purée the 1¼ pounds berries in a food processor, and, again, press through a fine sieve. Put the strained purée into a bowl, and sprinkle the gelatin into it. Blend well; set the purée aside.

- Whip the yolks and sugar until light and slightly thickened.
- In a saucepan heat the milk and vanilla to scalding, then slowly, steadily pour the hot milk into the yolks, whipping constantly. Return the mixture to the sauce pan. Cook it over a medium flame, while stirring constantly, until it is smooth and thickened. Stir in the raspberry-gelatin mixture. Transfer the bavarian cream to a stainless steel bowl, and place the bowl in an ice bath. Stir until the bavarian cream is well chilled and beginning to set. Fold in the whipped cream with a rubber spatula until completely blended.
- Fill a bavarian or charlotte mold with cold water. Pour out the water, and shake out the excess, but leave the mold damp. Fill it with the bavarian cream. Cover the mold, and chill overnight.
- Dip the mold into very hot water, pat it dry, then invert it onto a platter. Chill the bavarian cream before serving.

(GARNISH)
- Decorate the dish with fresh mint and fresh raspberries. Serve the raspberry sauce separately.

Strawberries Romanoff

⅓ cup Grand Marnier
3 tablespoons sugar
1 pint fresh strawberries, their tops removed, gently rinsed and split in half

¼ cup vodka
1 cup heavy cream
1 tablespoon sugar
1 sprig mint

Cookbook authors differ on the type of liqueur used for marinating the strawberries in Strawberries Romanoff. Our recipe is nearly identical to the original, created for the Romanoff aristocracy in Russia during the nineteenth century. Some recipes we have seen call for kirschwasser and maraschino liqueur. Others call for brandy or cognac. Feel free to substitute any liqueur that pleases your palate.

- Combine the Grand Marnier, vodka, and 2 tablespoons sugar. Add the strawberry halves. Cover, and place in the refrigerator to marinate for 3 to 4 hours.
- Whip the heavy cream with 1 tablespoon sugar until the cream forms stiff peaks.
- Spoon the strawberries out of the marinating liquid, and fold them into the whipped cream. Spoon the strawberries and cream into individual bowls, and garnish with mint leaves.

Apple Strudel

Strudel dough (page 21) or 1 1-pound package commercial *phyllo* dough
6 ounces unsalted butter
2 cups fresh white bread crumbs
approximately 12 Granny Smith or other crisp, tart apples

juice of 2 lemons
¾ cup raisins
½ cup chopped walnuts
1¼ cups sugar
1½ teaspoons ground cinnamon
confectionary sugar

- Place 2 ounces of the butter in a large skillet or sauté pan. Add the bread crumbs, and stir over a medium flame until the crumbs are golden brown. Set the pan aside.
- Peel the apples with a vegetable peeler. Cut them in half lengthwise, and remove their cores with a parisienne scoop. To prevent the apples from browning, place them in a large bowl with the lemon juice and enough cold water to cover. When all the apples have been peeled and cored, cut them into thin slices, and return them to the lemon water. Set the bowl aside.
- With the dough spread on a 3-by-3-foot floured cloth (see page 21), brush the surface with 2 ounces butter, melted. Sprinkle the toasted bread crumbs over.
- Remove the apple slices from the lemon water, and pat them dry. Put them into a large bowl along with the raisins, walnuts, sugar, and cinnamon. Stir together.
- Preheat an oven to 400°F.
- Spoon the apple mixture down one side of the dough, about 2 inches from the edge. Lift the cloth beneath this edge, and begin rolling the dough over the filling. Fold in the two ends to enclose the apple filling, and continue rolling and folding in the ends until the strudel is completely rolled up. Place the strudel on a baking sheet, either lightly greased or covered with a sheet of parchment paper.
- Melt the remaining butter, and brush the strudel with it. Bake 35 to 40 minutes, or until the strudel is golden brown. Allow it to cool at least 15 minutes before slicing.
- Dust with confectionary sugar upon serving. Serves 12.

Apple Pie with Vermont Cheese

(PASTRY)

4 cups flour
12 ounces unsalted butter, cut
　　into ½-inch cubes
½ teaspoon salt

1 teaspoon sugar
½ cup cold water
1 large egg

(FILLING)

3 pounds tart cooking apples,
　　such as Granny Smith,
　　Rhode Island Greenings, or
　　Gravenstein
juice of 1 lemon
¼ cup sugar

1 tablespoon cornstarch
½ teaspoon cinnamon
¼ teaspoon nutmeg
2 tablespoons brandy
zest of 1 lemon
½ cup raisins (optional)

(TO ASSEMBLE)

the pastry
the filling
1 egg, beaten
1 tablespoon sugar

sharp white Vermont cheddar
　　cheese, in slices 3 inches by
　　2 inches by ¼ inch

(PASTRY)

♦ Combine the flour, butter, salt, and sugar in a large bowl. Rub the ingredients between your hands, until the butter is broken up and distributed evenly throughout the dry ingredients. Stir in the water and egg, and press the dough into a ball. Refrigerate it 15 minutes.

♦ Divide the dough into 2 parts. Roll out one portion about $3/16$-inch thick on a floured board. Gently fold the dough in half. Brush excess flour from the dough, then carefully place it in a lightly buttered 10-inch pie pan. Leave the excess dough hanging over the edges of the pan. Roll out the second ball of dough to roughly the same thickness, and set both portions aside.

♦ Preheat an oven to 375°F.

(FILLING)

♦ Peel the apples, cut them in half lengthwise, and remove their cores. To prevent the apples from browning, place them in a large bowl with the lemon juice and enough cold water to cover. When all the apples have been peeled and cored, cut them into thin slices, and return them to the lemon water.

♦ Drain the apples, and put them into a large bowl. Add the sugar, cornstarch, cinnamon, nutmeg, brandy, lemon zest, and raisins (if desired). Gently toss to combine all ingredients.

(TO ASSEMBLE)

♦ Fill the pie pan with the apple mixture. Cover with the second sheet of dough. Trim off the excess dough, and press and crimp the edges together. Brush the top of the pie with the egg wash, and sprinkle lightly with sugar. Cut a small opening in the center of the pie to allow the steam to escape. Bake the pie 35 to 45 minutes, until it is golden brown. Allow it to cool 20 minutes. Serve it with sliced Vermont cheddar cheese.

♦ Makes 1 10-inch double-crust pie.

Grand Marnier Soufflé

(BATTER)

¼ pound unsalted butter	1½ teaspoons vanilla extract
½ cup flour, sifted	yolks of 4 large eggs
⅛ teaspoon salt	whites of 6 large eggs
2½ cups milk	5 tablespoons Grand Marnier
¾ cup sugar	

(TO PREPARE THE RAMEKINS)

unsalted butter	sugar

(SAUCE)

1 pint premium-quality vanilla ice cream	½ cup heavy cream
	¼ cup Grand Marnier

Be sure to be gentle when folding in the egg whites. The air whipped in to the whites is what causes the soufflé to rise. Rough handling would break down the whipped whites and impair this rising. It helps to use a rubber spatula and to do the folding in two parts.

Making a soufflé seems to be the quintessential culinary challenge, and a failed soufflé indicates a failed chef. When a soufflé fails to rise, or falls before the diner can cut into it, the cook can do little to remedy the situation. But by understanding the nature of a soufflé, and following the recipe exactly, you will have an excellent chance of success. Of course, it wouldn't hurt to have a spectacular backup dessert on hand, just in case.

(BATTER, STEP I)

♦ In a sauce pan, melt the butter. Add the flour and salt, and stir to blend. Continue stirring over low heat 2 to 3 minutes, until the flour emits a nutty aroma. *Do not brown.* Remove the mixture from the fire, and set it aside.

♦ In another sauce pan, scald the milk. Remove the pan from the fire. Stir in the sugar and the vanilla.

♦ Return the flour and butter mixture to the fire. Add the milk, stirring constantly as it comes to a simmer and thickens. Continue stirring and simmering until the mixture is fully thickened. Remove it from the fire, and strain it into a mixing bowl. Allow it to cool for 15 minutes.

♦ Add the egg yolks one at a time, stirring in each yolk before adding the next. Add the Grand Marnier, and set the mixture aside.

(TO PREPARE THE RAMEKINS)

♦ Coat the insides of four 8-ounce ovenproof ramekins with butter. Fill a buttered ramekin with about ¼ cup of sugar, and rotate the dish until all the butter is coated with sugar. Gently tap out the sugar into another ramekin, and rotate the second dish until the butter is lightly coated with sugar. Repeat with the remaining ramekins, then refrigerate the dishes until you are ready to fill them.

♦ Preheat an oven to 400°F.

♦ Take the ice cream from the freezer to allow it to soften.

(BATTER, STEP II)

♦ Whip the egg whites in a clean bowl until they hold a stiff peak. *Gently* fold the whites, one-half at a time, into the butter, flour, and milk mixture. *Do not overmix.* When all the egg whites are incorporated, divide the soufflé batter among the prepared ramekins. The batter should be level with the top edge of each ramekin.

♦ Place the ramekins on a baking sheet, about 2 inches apart. Bake 18 minutes, or until the soufflés are fully risen and golden brown on top.

(SAUCE)

♦ While the soufflés are baking, combine the ice cream, heavy cream, and Grand Marnier in a bowl. Stir to blend well. Transfer the sauce to a gooseneck or other sauce dish.

♦ Serve the soufflés directly from the oven on underliner plates, topped with some of the sauce.

MISCELLANEOUS

Marjolaine

Hazelnut praline paste is available at any good confectionary or gourmet shop, and, in large quantities, at restaurant supply outlets.

(SPONGE CAKE)

4½ ounces (about 1 cup) sliced almonds
12½ tablespoons sugar
3 large eggs

3½ tablespoons flour
whites of 3 large eggs
pinch salt
1½ tablespoons melted butter

(GANACHE)

10½ ounces semisweet chocolate

1 cup heavy cream
2 ounces unsalted butter

(NUT MERINGUE)

¾ cup almonds
1½ tablespoons cornstarch
½ cup sugar

whites of 4 large eggs
pinch salt
2 tablespoons sugar

(BUTTERCREAM)

4 eggs
⅓ cup sugar
1 cup milk
1 pound unsalted butter, softened

2 ounces (about 4 tablespoons) hazelnut praline paste
2 ounces semisweet chocolate, melted

(TO ASSEMBLE)

the sponge cake halves
the ganache, divided in half
the meringue halves

the chocolate buttercream
the hazelnut buttercream
cocoa powder

(SPONGE CAKE)

♦ Pulverize the sliced almonds with 10 tablespoons sugar in a food processor until very fine. Beat the eggs in a mixing bowl until light and creamy. To the eggs add the pulverized nuts and sugar and the sifted flour. Stir gently until all are blended.

♦ Lightly butter the bottom of an 11-by-17-inch sheet pan. Cut a piece of parchment or wax paper to fit the bottom of the pan. Lay the paper in the pan, then lightly butter the paper.

♦ Preheat an oven to 350°F.

♦ Beat the egg whites with the salt to soft peaks. Slowly add 2½ tablespoons sugar, while beating, and continue beating to stiff peaks.

♦ Fold first the melted butter, then the egg whites, into the batter. Spread the batter evenly in the sheet pan. Bake 8 to 10 minutes. Allow the cake to cool, then invert it onto a work surface and cut it in half horizontally. Set the two parts aside.

(GANACHE)
- Melt the chocolate, cream, and butter in a double boiler. Stir until the ingredients are well blended. Chill the mixture 1½ hours.

(NUT MERINGUE)
- Lightly butter and paper an 11-by-17-inch sheet pan in the same manner as for the sponge cake.
- Preheat an oven to 225°F.
- Pulverize the almonds with the cornstarch and sugar in a food processor. Beat the whites with the salt to soft peaks. While beating, add the 2 tablespoons sugar; continue beating to stiff peaks. Fold the whites into the almond mixture, one-half at a time.
- Spread the meringue on the greased sheet, and bake 40 minutes, or until the meringue is firm and slightly brown. Remove the pan from the oven, allow the meringue to cool 5 minutes, and invert it onto a work surface. Cut the meringue in half horizontally, and set it aside to cool fully.

(BUTTERCREAM)
- Beat the eggs and the sugar until light and frothy. In a sauce pan scald the milk, then pour the egg-sugar mixture slowly into the hot milk, while continuously stirring. Heat and stir vigorously until the mixture is thick and creamy. Set it aside, and allow it to cool.
- Beat the butter in an electric mixer until it is smooth and creamy. Divide it in half, and put the two halves into two separate bowls. Beat the hazelnut praline paste into one, and the melted chocolate into the other, until both mixtures are completely blended. Divide the cooled milk-egg mixture in half, and beat half into each of the two butter mixtures. Set the mixtures aside.

(TO ASSEMBLE)
- Place one of the sponge cake halves on a work surface. Spread half the *ganache* evenly over the cake. Top with a layer of meringue. Spread the chocolate buttercream over this, then top with the second layer of sponge cake. Spread the hazelnut buttercream over the cake, and top with the second layer of meringue. Spread the remaining *ganache* over the meringue. Trim the edges square with a serrated knife, and lightly dust with cocoa powder. Chill at least 2 hours before serving.

Chiffon Pumpkin Pie

(PIE CRUST)

3 cups flour
½ cup sugar
¼ teaspoon salt
10 ounces butter, cut into ½-inch cubes, and softened to room temperature

1 egg plus 1 yolk, slightly beaten

(CHIFFON FILLING)

2 teaspoons unflavored granulated gelatin
3½ ounces (scant ½ cup) cold water
2 large eggs, separated
pinch salt

½ cup sugar
3 ounces (⅓ cup) canned pumpkin
⅓ teaspoon cinnamon
⅛ teaspoon ginger
pinch nutmeg

(GARNISH)

1½ cups heavy cream

¼ cup sugar

(PIE CRUST)

- Put the flour, sugar, and salt into a large mixing bowl. Add the butter cubes, and rub this mixture between your hands until the butter is broken up and evenly distributed among the dry ingredients.
- Add the beaten eggs, blend with a rotary mixer, and press the dough into a large ball. Wrap the dough in plastic, and place it in the refrigerator to chill 30 minutes.
- Preheat an oven to 375°F.
- On a floured board, roll out half the dough in a circle large enough to fit a 9- or 10-inch pie pan or tart form. Press the dough into the pan or tart form, and dock it (pierce it all over with the tines of a fork). Place the pie shell in the refrigerator to chill 15 minutes. Wrap and freeze the remaining dough for later use.
- Bake the pie shell at 375°F for 15 minutes. Remove it from the oven, and set it aside to cool.

(CHIFFON FILLING)

- In a sauce pan, sprinkle the gelatin into the cold water. Stir the mixture over a medium flame until the gelatin has dissolved and the liquid is clear.
- Put the 2 egg yolks into a small bowl, and whip them in a double boiler until they are light and frothy (be careful not to overcook them; they could turn into scrambled eggs). Remove them from the heat, and whip in the gelatin water, pumpkin, and spices.
- In another bowl, whip the egg whites with the salt. Pour in the sugar while beating. Beat to soft peaks.

- Fold the egg whites into the pumpkin mixture, and pour this filling into the cooled pie shell. Smooth the top and refrigerate the pie.

(GARNISH)
- Whip the heavy cream to stiff peaks, incorporating the sugar while whipping. Fit a pastry bag with a #7 star tip, and fill the bag with the whipped cream (see page 16). Pipe rosettes or stars onto the top of the chiffon pie. Chill at least one more hour before serving. Makes 1 pie, to serve 8.

Pecan Tart with Bourbon Sauce

(PASTRY)

5⅓ ounces unsalted butter, softened	1⅓ cups flour
3½ ounces (about ⅓ cup) cream cheese, softened	

(FILLING)

3 large eggs	pinch salt
⅓ cup molasses	½ teaspoon vanilla extract
3 tablespoons light corn syrup	¼ cup plus 2 tablespoons flour
2 ounces butter, melted	2¼ cups pecan halves

(BOURBON SAUCE)

1 quart heavy cream	¼ cup bourbon
1½ tablespoons sugar	

(PASTRY)
- Beat the butter and cream cheese in an electric mixer until light and smooth. Add the flour, and beat until it is completely incorporated.
- Roll out the dough on a floured board. Carefully press it into a 10-inch tart form with a removable bottom. Chill the pastry shell in the refrigerator until you are ready to fill it.

(FILLING)
- Preheat an oven to 375°F.
- In an electric mixer, beat the eggs until they are light and frothy. Add the molasses, syrup, butter, salt, and vanilla, and whip in. Add the flour, and mix until smooth. Stir in the pecans, then pour the mixture into the pastry shell.
- Bake the tart 40 minutes. Makes one 10-inch tart.

(BOURBON SAUCE)
- Combine the cream and the sugar in a sauce pan, and reduce by half. Stir in the bourbon. Serve the sauce hot, on the side, with the heated tart.

Hazelnut Torte

(CAKE)

6 large eggs, separated
½ cup sugar
1½ tablespoons lemon juice
2 teaspoons lemon zest

¼ cup graham cracker crumbs
6 ounces (about 1¼ cups) fine-
    ground hazelnuts
pinch salt

(COOKIE DOUGH)

3 cups flour
¼ teaspoon salt
½ cup sugar
10 ounces unsalted butter, cut
    into ½-inch cubes

1 large egg
yolk of 1 large egg

(BUTTERCREAM)

1½ cups sugar
¾ cup water
whites of 7 large eggs

12 ounces unsalted butter,
    softened
dash vanilla extract

(TO ASSEMBLE)

the cookie circle
currant jelly
the three cake rounds
the buttercream
1 cup fine-ground toasted
    hazelnuts

4 ounces (about 1 cup) whole
    toasted hazelnuts
3 ounces chocolate

(CAKE)

- Beat the yolks with the sugar until light and slightly thickened.
  Add the lemon juice, zest, graham cracker crumbs, and nuts,
  and blend.
- Preheat an oven to 350°F.
- Whip the whites with the salt to stiff peaks. Fold the whites into
  the batter, one-half at a time.
- Transfer the batter to a greased and lightly floured 9-inch cake
  pan. Bake 25 to 30 minutes, or until the cake pulls away from
  the sides of the pan. Cool the cake in the pan for 10 minutes,
  then turn it out onto a rack.

(COOKIE DOUGH)

- Combine the flour, salt, sugar, and butter cubes in a small mixing
  bowl. Mash the mixture with your fingers until the butter is well
  distributed. Beat the egg and the yolk together, add them to the
  dough, and blend thoroughly with a rotary mixer. Refrigerate
  15 minutes.
- Preheat an oven to 350°F.
- Roll out the dough on a floured surface into a circle slightly
  larger than 9 inches. Set the 9-inch cake pan on top of the dough,
  and cut a perfect 9-inch circle. Place the circle on a greased

baking sheet, and bake it 15 to 20 minutes, or until it is golden brown. Allow it to cool to room temperature.

(BUTTERCREAM)

♦ Cook the sugar and the water to 238°F, using a pastry thermometer to check the temperature. Remove the pan from the fire.
♦ Beat the egg whites to soft peaks.
♦ Pour the hot syrup slowly into the egg whites, while beating constantly. Allow the mixture to cool. Add the softened butter and the vanilla, and beat until the buttercream is smooth and creamy.

(TO ASSEMBLE)

♦ Place the 9-inch cookie base on a 9-inch corrugated cardboard circle. Spread with a thin layer of currant jelly. Cut the cake horizontally into three equal rounds. Place one of these rounds on the jelly-coated cookie base. Top with a layer of buttercream. Place a second cake round on top of this, and top again with a layer of buttercream. Place the third cake round on top. Cover the entire structure with the buttercream. With one hand, lift the torte on its cardboard circle. With the other hand, gently press the ground toasted hazelnuts all around the side of the torte.
♦ Fill a pastry bag, fitted with a #7 star tip, with the remaining buttercream (see page 16). Pipe out 16 buttercream rosettes around the top edge of the torte. Place a toasted hazelnut on each rosette.
♦ Melt the chocolate in a double boiler. Put the melted chocolate into another pastry bag, fitted with a #2 round pastry tip, and pipe onto the torte 2 sets of parallel lines at right angles to each other. Chill the torte at least 2 hours before serving.

Rum and Ginger Mousse

Crystallized ginger is a ginger-flavored candy with a texture much like gum drops. It is available in any good gourmet, confectionary, or Asian food shop.

1½ cups milk
1¼-ounce package unflavored granulated gelatin
¼ cup plus 3 tablespoons sugar
1 tablespoon grated fresh ginger

2 teaspoons cornstarch
1½ tablespoons dark rum
2 medium eggs, separated
⅓ plus ¼ cup heavy cream
4 pieces crystallized ginger

♦ Combine the milk, gelatin, and ¼ cup sugar in a sauce pan. Heat and stir until the gelatin is dissolved. Add the ginger. Dissolve the cornstarch in the rum, and add this mixture to the hot milk. Cook and stir 15 seconds or so, until the cornstarch has thickened. Remove the pan from the fire.
♦ Beat the egg yolks until they are light and slightly thickened.

While continuously beating, slowly stir the milk mixture into the egg yolks. Return the mixture to the sauce pan, and heat it, while beating, for 5 minutes. Remove it from the fire, and allow it to cool.

- Beat the whites to soft peaks. Add 1½ tablespoons sugar, while beating, and continue beating to stiff peaks. Fold the whites into the cooled milk mixture.
- Beat ⅓ cup cream with 1½ tablespoons sugar to stiff peaks. Fold the cream into the mousse mixture. Pour the mousse into wine glasses, and chill at least 2 hours.
- Before serving, whip the ¼ cup cream. Garnish each glass with a whipped cream rosette (use a #8 or #9 star tip) and crystallized ginger.

Baked Rice Pudding with Fruit

1 quart milk	1 large egg
1 vanilla bean, split (or 1 teaspoon vanilla extract)	yolks of 2 large eggs
1 cup sugar	1 pint milk
¼ teaspoon salt	½ teaspoon cinnamon
⅔ cup white long-grain rice	½ cup heavy cream, whipped
¾ cup raisins	2 cups fresh fruit of your choice, such as apples, pears, apricots, peaches, or berries
1 cup hot water	

- Put the milk, vanilla bean or extract, sugar, salt, and rice into a saucepan. While stirring, bring to a boil. Cover the pan, turn down the flame, and simmer 30 minutes, until the rice has completely absorbed the milk.
- Soak the raisins 30 minutes in the hot water. Drain.
- Preheat the oven to 400°F.
- Beat the eggs and yolks together until they are light and slightly thickened. Scald the pint of milk, and slowly pour it into the beaten eggs, while continuously whipping. Stir this mixture into the rice. Stir in the raisins.
- Transfer the pudding mixture to a lightly buttered 1½- to 2-quart casserole dish. Bake the pudding 20 minutes. Stir the pudding, sprinkle the cinnamon over it, and bake another 20 minutes. Serve hot with whipped cream and your choice of fresh fruit.

Cream Puff Swans

2 ounces butter	1 medium egg, beaten with a tablespoon of water
½ cup water	1 cup heavy cream
⅛ teaspoon salt	2 tablespoons sugar
½ cup flour	confectionary sugar
2 large eggs	

The French term for cream puff dough is pâte à choux. Pâte *means "paste," or "dough";* choux *means "cabbage." The dough got its name because a baked cream puff looks like a little cabbage.*

- In a sauce pan, bring the butter, water, and salt to a rolling boil. When the butter has completely melted, remove the pan from the fire, and add the flour. Stir until all ingredients are blended and the dough comes away from the sides of the pan. Adjust the amount of flour if necessary. Allow the dough to cool.
- Add the eggs to the cooled dough one at a time, blending the first in completely before adding the second.
- Preheat an oven to 400°F.
- Fit a pastry bag with a #7 round tip. Fill the pastry bag with about two-thirds of the dough (see page 16). Pipe teardrop shaped pieces, about 2½ inches across at their widest point, onto a baking pan that is lightly buttered or covered with a sheet of parchment paper. Pipe out teardrops until the pastry bag is empty.
- Fit another pastry bag with a #5 round tip. Fill the bag with the remaining dough, and pipe out 2½-inch-long pieces in the shape of question marks. Again, pipe until the bag is empty. Lightly brush all the dough pieces with the egg wash.
- Bake the dough pieces at 400°F for about 15 minutes, or until they are puffed and golden brown.
- Remove the pan from the oven, and allow the pieces to cool to room temperature. With a serrated knife, horizontally halve four of the best-looking, most puffy teardrops. Cut the top halves in two, and set these aside with the bottom halves.
- Whip the cream to stiff peaks, adding the sugar as you do so. Fill a pastry bag fitted with a #7 star tip. Pipe the whipped cream into the bottom halves of the sliced teardrops. For each swan, stick the two pieces of the severed top into the cream, to imitate wings. Then insert one of the question mark shapes, to look like the swan's neck and head. Dust each swan with confectionary sugar, chill, and serve.

Crème Brulée

(CRÈME)
3 large eggs
yolks of 3 large eggs
½ cup plus ⅓ cup sugar

2 tablespoons Grand Marnier
1 pint heavy cream
1 teaspoon vanilla extract

(TOPPING)
¼ cup brown sugar

¼ cup sugar

(CRÈME)
- Whip the eggs, yolks, ½ cup sugar, and Grand Marnier in a blender until light and doubled in volume.
- In a sauce pan, scald the cream, vanilla, and ⅓ cup sugar.
- Turn the blender on low speed, and slowly pour the cream mixture into the eggs. Return the mixture to the sauce pan, and cook it over medium heat, while stirring constantly, until it is

thick and smooth. Transfer the *crème* to four 8-ounce ovenproof ramekins, soup cups, or soufflé dishes.

(TOPPING)
- Mix the sugar and brown sugar together, and sprinkle over each dish. Set the dishes under a broiler until the sugars melt and turn golden brown.
- Remove the dishes, and let them cool to room temperature. Cover and refrigerate them until you are ready to serve.

ICE CREAM AND SORBETS

Pear Sorbet

2 cups water
½ cup sugar
6 medium pears

¼ cup lemon juice
¼ cup pear liqueur
8–10 sprigs mint

- Bring the water and sugar to a boil. Cook until the sugar is fully dissolved. Remove the syrup from the fire, and allow it to cool.
- Put ¼ cup of the sugar syrup, along with the lemon juice, into a skillet or sauté pan.
- Peel the pears with a vegetable peeler. Cut them in half lengthwise, and remove their cores with a parisienne scoop. Cut the halves into rough pieces, dropping the pieces immediately into the syrup and lemon juice to prevent browning. When the pears have all been cut up, simmer the pieces in the sugar syrup and lemon juice until they are very tender. Remove the pan from the fire, and allow the pears to cool.
- Purée the pears along with the syrup in which they were cooked. Press the purée through a sieve into a bowl. Stir in the remaining syrup and the pear liqueur. Put the bowl in a freezer, and stir the sorbet four times, at 20-minute intervals. Then leave it alone to freeze fully. This should take 2 hours.
- Serve the sorbet garnished with sprigs of fresh mint. Makes 8 to 10 servings.

Strawberry-Cassis Sorbet

4 pints fresh strawberries,
    rinsed, their tops removed
¼ cup plus 1 tablespoon sugar
1 cup water

½ cup crème de cassis
8–10 sprigs mint
2 tablespoons lemon juice

- In a large mixing bowl, mash the berries and 1 tablespoon sugar with a fork. Allow the mashed berries to stand 1 hour.
- Bring the water and ¼ cup sugar to a boil, and cook until the sugar is fully dissolved. Remove the pan from the fire, allow the syrup to cool, then refrigerate it.
- Press the mashed berries, along with their juice, through a sieve. Combine this purée, the chilled syrup, the cassis, and the lemon juice. Strain the entire mixture through the sieve into a bowl. Put the bowl into the freezer, and stir the sorbet four times, at 20-minute intervals. Then leave it alone for about 2 hours, to freeze fully.
- Serve the sorbet garnished with fresh mint. Makes 8 to 10 servings.

Mango Sorbet

3 cups water
1 cup sugar
6 very ripe mangos
¼ cup lemon juice

¼ cup Cointreau or other
   orange liqueur
10–12 sprigs mint

- Bring the water and sugar to a boil, and simmer until the sugar is dissolved. Let the syrup cool, then refrigerate it.
- Peel the mangos, and cut the flesh away from the pits. Purée the flesh in a food processor.
- Combine the mango purée, the chilled syrup, the lemon juice, and the liqueur. Press the mixture through a sieve into a bowl. Put the bowl in a freezer, and stir the sorbet four times, at 20-minute intervals. Then leave it alone to freeze fully. This will take about 2 hours.
- Serve garnished with fresh mint. Makes 10 to 12 servings.

Amaretti-Rum Ice Cream

Unlike sorbet, ice cream cannot be made without an ice cream machine. Many models are available, both manually and electrically operated. If you are an ice cream aficionado, we recommend you invest in an electric machine. There is nothing quite like homemade ice cream.

1 cup water
¾ cup sugar
8 egg yolks
1 cup heavy cream

⅔ cup coarsely chopped
   amaretti di Saronna (or
   similar) cookies
6 tablespoons light rum

- Bring the water and sugar to a boil in a sauce pan. Remove the pan from the fire.
- In a small bowl beat the yolks until they are thickened and doubled in volume. While still beating, very slowly pour the hot syrup into the yolks, in a thin, steady stream. Remove this mixture to a sauce pan, and, while stirring constantly, cook it until it thickens. Transfer it to a clean bowl, cover the bowl, and allow the mixture to cool completely.

- Whip the cream to stiff peaks. Fold the whipped cream and cookie pieces into the cooled yolk mixture. Refrigerate the complete mixture 45 minutes.
- Transfer the mixture to an ice cream maker. Add the rum while processing. Put the ice cream in the freezer to harden; this will take at least 2 hours.
- Makes 1 quart.

Coffee Ice Cream

2 cups half and half
1 cup sugar
¾ cup coffee beans, coarsely ground

2 ounces unsalted butter
yolks of 6 large eggs
1 cup heavy cream

- In a sauce pan, bring to a boil the half and half, sugar, ground coffee, and butter. Remove the pan from the fire, and allow it to sit 15 minutes. Strain the mixture through a fine sieve.
- Beat the yolks until they are slightly thickened and roughly doubled in volume. While still beating, add the heavy cream.
- Add the coffee mixture to the eggs and cream, and blend well.
- Put this mixture into a sauce pan over a medium flame, and, while stirring constantly, cook until it begins to thicken. *Do not let it boil*. Remove it from the heat, and allow it to cool. Cover it, and refrigerate it overnight.
- Transfer the ice cream to an ice cream machine, process it, and freeze it at least 2 hours. Makes 1 quart.

Praline Ice Cream

¾ cup sugar
2 tablespoons water
¾ cup almonds, hazelnuts, walnuts, or a combination of these, coarsely chopped

3 cups milk
⅓ cup sugar
6 egg yolks
3 tablespoons dark rum

- Combine the sugar, water, and nuts in a sauce pan. Stir and cook over medium heat until the sugar is lightly caramelized. Pour the praline onto a lightly oiled baking sheet. Allow it to cool and harden.
- Break the praline into coarse pieces, put them into a food processor, and pulverize them.
- Put the egg yolks and the sugar into the top of a double boiler over simmering water. Whip until they are slightly thickened and roughly doubled in volume. Remove the mixture from the heat.
- Scald the milk. Use a ladle to pour a slow, steady stream of hot

milk into the egg yolks, while beating. Return this mixture to the fire, and cook it over a medium flame, while stirring constantly. When it is thickened, remove it from the fire and allow it to cool. Stir in the ground praline, cover, and refrigerate overnight.

♦ When the mixture is fully chilled, add the dark rum, process in the ice cream machine, and freeze the ice cream at least 2 hours. Makes 1 quart.

INDEX

D

E

The Pillar House Cookbook was composed in Sabon, a typeface designed by Jan Tschichold. Basing the roman on a font engraved by Claude Garamond and the italic on a font by Robert Granjon, Tschichold introduced many refinements to make the model suitable for contemporary typographic needs. The book was composed by Crane Typesetting Service of Barnstable, Massachusetts, and printed and bound by Capital City Press of Montpelier, Vermont. The paper is 60-pound Glatfelter Antique Offset.

If you would like one or more copies of The Pillar House Cookbook by David Paul Larousse and Alan R. Gibson, please write to—

The Harvard Common Press
535 Albany Street
Boston, Massachusetts 02118

The Pillar House Cookbook is available in paperback for $14.95. When ordering, please enclose a check or money order for the full price plus $3.00 for postage and handling. If you are a Massachusetts resident, please add 5 percent sales tax.

The Harvard Common Press also publishes several other cookbooks. We would be happy to send you our catalogue at no charge. Just write us at the above address.